Inspiration for Interpreters

The National Association for Interpretation

The National Association for Interpretation (NAI) is a 501(c)(3) not-for-profit professional organization dedicated to advancing the profession of heritage interpretation, currently serving about 6,500 members in the United States and over thirty other nations. Individual members include those who work at parks, museums, nature centers, zoos, botanical gardens, aquariums, historical and cultural sites, commercial tour companies, and theme parks. Commercial and institutional members include those who provide services to the heritage interpretation industry. In accordance with NAI's mission statement, InterpPress publishes books that improve the profession of interpretation over the long term.

Inspiration for Interpreters

Moving Beyond the Treeline and Other Stories

Larry Beck

ROWMAN & LITTLEFIELD
Lanham • Boulder • New York • London

Published by Rowman & Littlefield
An imprint of The Rowman & Littlefield Publishing Group, Inc.
4501 Forbes Boulevard, Suite 200, Lanham, Maryland 20706
www.rowman.com

86-90 Paul Street, London EC2A 4NE

British Library Cataloguing in Publication Information Available

Library of Congress Cataloging-in-Publication Data

ISBN 979-8-8818-0299-8 (cloth : alk. paper)
ISBN 979-8-8818-0300-1 (paper : alk. paper)
ISBN 979-8-8818-0301-8 (electronic)

♾™ The paper used in this publication meets the minimum requirements of American National Standard for Information Sciences—Permanence of Paper for Printed Library Materials, ANSI/NISO Z39.48-1992.

Let us probe the silent places,

let us seek what luck betide us;

Let us journey to a lonely land I know.

There's a whisper on the night wind,

there's a star agleam to guide us,

And the Wild is calling, calling … let us go.

—Robert Service

For Leo McAvoy, a former Navy navigator, and Al Gustaveson, a former merchant marine, for their leadership and passion for open water.

For long-time friend and colleague Dan Dustin.

And for Vicki.

Contents

Foreword ix

Acknowledgments xi

A Brief Personal History and an Introduction to the Stories 1

Part I: Moving Beyond the Treeline

Prologue: First Nations 13

Chapter 1: Voyageurs 17

Chapter 2: Paddling 21

Chapter 3: Olesen's Place 29

Chapter 4: Portaging 33

Chapter 5: Aki 39

Chapter 6: A Complete Desolation, a Northern Fairyland 41

Chapter 7: No Rescue Wilderness 45

Chapter 8: The Country, the Space, the Sky 51

Chapter 9: Wolf Pups 55

Chapter 10: The Way of Adventure 57

Part II: And Other Stories

Barry Lopez: Leading by Story   63

Running for Our Lives   67

Reality Matters: Larry Beck and Dan Dustin   71

Keeping Our Democracy Intact   77

Interpreting New York City's Missing Towers   83

Interpreting Hope   89

References and Notes   93
About the Author   99

Foreword

If you've ever walked the winding paths of the field of interpretation, chances are you've heard the name Larry Beck whispered with reverence. For over fifty years, Larry has not just walked these paths—he's paved them, planted gardens of insight along the way, and built bridges where none existed before. As an interpreter at some of the most iconic sites and a professor at San Diego State University, Larry has dedicated his life to not just teaching interpretation, but transforming it.

Larry's books have been the North Star for countless interpreters, guiding them through the intricate dance of cultural and natural resource interpretation. Starting with the seminal *Interpretation of Cultural and Natural Resources* in 1995, coauthored with Douglas M. Knudson and Ted Cable, Larry has consistently provided the tools and inspiration needed to excel in this field. His subsequent works, *The Gifts of Interpretation*, *Interpretive Perspectives*, and *Interpreting Cultural and Natural Heritage*, have cemented his status as a cornerstone of interpretive literature.

Larry Beck's influence cannot be contained within the pages of his books or the impressive array of awards he's received. Yes, he's got the National Association for Interpretation's Meritorious Service Award, the prestigious Fellow Award, and the President's Award. However, the legacy I most admire Larry for is advocacy for social justice. From 2018 to 2024, Larry penned a groundbreaking twenty-eight-part series for NAI's *Legacy* magazine called *Justice for All*. This series didn't just scratch the surface; it dug deep into the heart of interpretation's role in amplifying marginalized voices. Whether it's telling the stories of Black Americans, Native Americans, women, persons with disabilities, LGBTQ+ individuals, or Japanese Americans, Larry's work has ensured that these narratives are not just told, but celebrated. This collection includes some of those pivotal articles, updated and as powerful as ever.

Larry's commitment to diversity and inclusion extends beyond his writing. Whenever NAI calls for donations to support scholarships and grants for underrepresented communities, Larry is first in line, credit card at the ready. True to form, he isn't pocketing a dime from this book. Instead, he reached out to NAI with a prewritten manuscript, then cheerfully revised and expanded it, with all royalties going to support NAI's mission.

Larry Beck doesn't just ask us to be good interpreters; he challenges us to be great humans. He urges us to advocate for those whose voices go unheard, to tackle the tough stories head-on, and to be beacons of hope in a world that often feels dark. His work is a call to action, a reminder that interpretation isn't just a profession—it's a force for good in a world that desperately needs us. His work inspires hope as an antidote to political extremism and a global climate crisis.

As we present this title, the first in NAI's new series with Rowman & Littlefield, I find myself filled with gratitude. Thank you, Larry, for your unparalleled contributions to interpretation, for your dedication to social justice, and for reminding us all that the paths we walk are not just for us, but for everyone.

Parker McMullen Bushman
President, National Association for Interpretation
May 2024

Acknowledgments

As I composed the brief personal history at the beginning of this book, I considered the countless people who have influenced my life. Listing everyone, of course, would be impossible. But those at the top of the list include my parents, Lou and Adelle Beck; my siblings, Joycee and David Beck; and my two sons, Spencer and Benjamin Beck. All are aware of my devotion to writing in the field of interpretation and have read much of my work. Long conversations with Spencer often influence the direction of my writing, and Joycee, a professional magician, has been able to work "magic" with my writing projects.

From the longer title essay "Moving Beyond the Treeline," I thank Dave and Kristen Olesen for their hospitality and for opening their lives to us. At the time of our canoe expedition, they were recently married. At this writing they now have two grown daughters who they raised at their remote cabin. Several friends and colleagues reviewed that original manuscript for accuracy and to provide editorial assistance, including Eric Blehm, Ted Cable, Dan Dustin, Gene Lamke, Leo McAvoy, and Chris and Jeff Lashmet.

Most of the "And Other Stories" fell under the editorial guidance of Paul Caputo prior to publication in various themed issues of *Legacy*. I have enjoyed both a professional relationship and friendship with Paul for more than twenty years. Paul traveled from Fort Collins, Colorado, to San Diego and back in one day to attend my retirement celebration in 2023. More recently I've enjoyed working with Lucien Meadows, the current editor of *Legacy*, on articles, one of which concludes the book, "Interpreting Hope." In addition to Paul and Lucien, I appreciate all the *Legacy* associate editors who have provided editorial assistance.

Over the course of more than forty years of teaching at San Diego State University several of my students have become friends. Two of those appear in the "Running for Our Lives" essay, Carol Morris and Amanda Gossard. They are central to that story, reviewed the draft article, and provided photos used in the original publication. Other friends have reviewed my articles, including Jim Lustig, Jason Hemmens, Tamara Brown, Andrea Saltzman, and Scott Gediman, and, as listed earlier, Dan Dustin and Ted Cable.

Authors often save their beloved for last, as the most important, in a listing of acknowledgments, and I have done the same. Vicki Fielden helped me in *moving beyond* a very troublesome time in my life. Over the past decade-plus she has traveled with me during all my field research, offered keen insights, and has always been the first to review my draft articles. Vicki is supportive in ways I hadn't known before. She is my best friend and confirms for me that life is sweeter when *lovingly* shared.

Acknowledgments

A Brief Personal History and an Introduction to the Stories

I am pleased to be part of the new arrangement between the National Association for Interpretation (NAI) and the well-established publishers Rowman & Littlefield. The publication guidelines focus on books that improve the profession of interpretation over the long term, and that might include samples of interpretive writing, the history of the field, trends within the field, and creative contributions offering fresh perspectives.

I hope to offer a little bit of all these things, starting with a brief modern history of the field from a personal lens. I find myself among a handful of people—such as Ted Cable, Sam Ham, and Tim Merriman—who have devoted half a century or more to working as field interpreters initially, and then trying to further understand the field, through research, teaching, and writing. The field has expanded dramatically over these past fifty years, and it has been an honor to be a part of that. My contribution to the profession has primarily been my writing.

As a child, I published a letter to the editor of our local *Riverside Press-Enterprise* in California arguing against a proposed shopping mall in the wild hills where I explored near my home. The shopping mall was built despite my impeccable logic and continues to be an eyesore to this day. But I was not deterred. I believed in the adage that the pen is mightier than the sword. Now, as an adult living in San Diego for several decades, I have written countless letters to the editor, opinion pieces, editorials, and commentaries for the *San Diego Union-Tribune*.

My career in interpretation began in the early 1970s when I was employed by the Riverside County Parks Department in California. A supervisor introduced me to Freeman Tilden's (1957) *Interpreting Our Heritage*, a book I treasured.

I then worked as an interpreter for the National Park Service in Alaska, California, Arizona, and Utah. I also worked for the Bureau of Land Management as a river ranger on the San Juan River in Utah, a "miniature" Grand Canyon, which included river patrol and interpretive duties. Although I loved my work, I chose to continue my education, earning a PhD at the University of Minnesota. That led to a faculty position at San Diego State University where I taught and conducted research over the next four decades.

My affiliation with NAI came when the Western Interpreters Association merged with the Association of Interpretive Naturalists in 1988 to form the National Association for Interpretation. The national conference that year was conveniently held in San Diego. I served on the conference planning committee and was chair of the research symposium. I have been a member of NAI ever since.

Very few books directly related to interpretation existed at the time. Then in the early 1990s Sam Ham's (1992) landmark book *Environmental Interpretation* was published, and that same year so was *The Interpreter's Guidebook* by Jim Buchholz, Brenda Lackey, Michael Gross, and Ron Zimmerman (one of many titles in the Interpreter's Handbook Series).

Around this same time, in the early 1990s, amid a budget crisis in California, I took a job at Kansas State University. Although I was only there for a semester, the experience was fortuitous because it was there that I met Ted Cable. The one comprehensive textbook for the profession, *Interpreting the Environment*, included a series of chapters by various authors, edited by Grant Sharpe (1976), but it went out of print. Ted had been working with Doug Knudson on a text that would cover all facets of heritage interpretation, a comprehensive resource for interpreters. Ted invited me to join the project, and it resulted in the first edition of our *Interpretation of Cultural and Natural Resources*, published in 1995. In 1996, Susan Strauss published *The Passionate Fact*, a book about interpretive storytelling. The interpretive profession's literature was growing.

Ted and I continued to write together. We decided to update and expand the existing interpretive principles. One of the key components of that project was to show that Enos Mills, who published *Adventures of a Nature Guide* in 1920, offered descriptions of proper interpretive guiding similar to Tilden's "six principles" in the first edition (1957) of *Interpreting Our Heritage*. We updated and built upon the principles that Mills and Tilden had written about, and we sought to move beyond those six principles by adding nine more. The first edition of our book, *Interpretation for the 21st Century: Fifteen Guiding Principles for Interpreting Nature and Culture*, was published in 1998 with an updated second edition in 2002.

Working with Paul Caputo, Ted and I published *Interpretive Perspectives*, a small book that contained selected essays we had written solo or as coauthors in *Legacy*, *The Interpreter*, *The Journal of Interpretation*, and the *Journal of Interpretation Research*. The essays appeared from 1989 to 2008, and the book was published in 2010. Paul wrote the foreword and noted that the pages of periodicals tend to be ephemeral compared to the longevity of a book, and that the selected essays "were collected and preserved for the benefit of the field of interpretation."

Throughout the early 2000s several books on various aspects of interpretation appeared titled *Personal Interpretation* (by Lisa Brochu and Tim Merriman in 2002), *Interpretive Planning* (by Lisa Brochu in 2003), and *Interpretive Writing* (by Alan Leftridge in 2006)—a deeper dive into some of the chapters covered in *Interpretation of Cultural and Natural Resources*. The literature continued to grow, and so did Ted's and my understanding of the importance of the profession.

As Ted and I prepared for a third edition of our "fifteen guiding principles," we associated each of the principles with a gift that interpreters share with their audiences. The book was retitled *The Gifts of Interpretation*, published in 2011, with each of our fifteen principles now associated with a gift such as a spark, provocation, wholeness, illumination, beauty, joy, passion, and hope. The most satisfying endorsement of the new book came from the foreword, written by Sam Ham, who remarked as he read through the book, "Yes. . . . This too is a gift." Referring to the first gift (The Gift of a Spark), Sam wrote, "Yes, the spark an interpreter might ignite in someone else is nothing short of a gift. It is given not only freely by the interpreter, but it is the potential to catalyze the spark that validates the interpreter's role in the first place."

Over the years, NAI increasingly became invested in the professional certification of interpreters. The most popular training was a one-week course leading to certification as a certified interpretive guide. One component of this course was a literature review. For many years, the text I coauthored with Doug and Ted, *Interpretation of Cultural and Natural Resources*, was part of that literature review, as was *The Gifts of Interpretation*, Tilden's *Interpreting Our Heritage*, a small book by Bill Lewis titled *Interpreting for Park Visitors*, *Personal Interpretation* by Lisa Brochu and Tim Merriman, and Sam Ham's *Environmental Interpretation* and then *Interpretation: Making a Difference on Purpose*. NAI also offered these books as a "Professional Certification Library Package," as they sought to ground future interpretive professionals in the seminal literature underpinning the profession.

In 2015, I led a two-and-a-half-year project with Ted and Doug to fully update our textbook, now titled *Interpreting Cultural and Natural Heritage: For a Better World*. At the conclusion of each chapter, we reflected on how the content of the chapter contributed to making the world a better place. We also enlisted the help of twenty-five luminaries in the field of interpretation to contribute "boxes" written about their specialty. Contributors included Sam Ham, Dan Dustin, Tim Merriman, Lisa Brochu, Paul Caputo, Mario Escalera, Alan Leftridge, Irene Rodriquez, and Chuck Lennox. Critical thinking about what the profession has to offer continued to expand.

AN INTERPRETIVE SEA CHANGE

At this point there was a discernable shift toward evolving interests in social and environmental justice. When the textbook project (*Interpreting Cultural and Natural Heritage: For a Better World*) concluded, I proposed a series of articles for NAI's *Legacy* magazine. I offered four articles to Paul Caputo, at that time the editor of *Legacy*, prior to his becoming the executive director of NAI. The project would focus primarily on marginalized communities and their contributions to our national story. I chose "Justice for All" as a banner for the column, which began in 2018. But then, after the first four articles, I just kept going. The series didn't end until the January/February 2024 issue of *Legacy*, almost six years, and twenty-eight articles, later.

In 2022, the editor and associate editors of *Legacy* devoted almost an entire year of thematic issues focused successively on justice, equity, diversity, accessibility, and inclusion (JEDAI) to highlight the organization's commitment to seeking justice, amplifying voices, representing underrepresented communities, advocating for diversity, and taking a stand on these important issues. This has now become an ethos that permeates NAI's culture.

Most recently, the theme of the January/February 2024 *Legacy* issue, "Uncomfortable Interpretation," was serendipitous in that I was able to write a retrospective about my "Justice for All" series, as well as six other feature articles I'd written, all of which fell under the broad umbrella of uncomfortable interpretation. My field research took me to places such as the Richmond Slave Trail in Virginia; Stonewall National Monument in Greenwich Village, New York City; the Chinese Laundry Building in Yosemite National Park; and the National Memorial for Peace and Justice (also referred to as the "lynching museum") in Montgomery, Alabama.

My retrospective was intended to shed light on why I started the "Justice for All" series in the first place, why I kept writing on these topics over the course of the next six years, what immersion in this subject matter and visiting interpretive sites all over the country meant to me, what it means to the profession, and what it means to the individual interpreter. I also made some provocative statements.

For example, I suggested that a willingness by interpreters to tackle uncomfortable topics may be the most important work interpreters can do. I wrote that because thousands of interpreters talk with millions of visitors to our interpretive sites every day, a willingness to enter a realm of potential discomfort could lead to "the saving of our democracy and the salvation of our planet."

The role of the interpreter, ultimately, is to promote the inherent dignity of all people and the sanctity of the land, with full and honest stories of our history and culture, and scientifically accurate portrayals of our relationship with nature. I noted that given the state of the world, this may, at times, be uncomfortable. I concluded with the words of Freedom Rider and longtime beloved congressman John Lewis, "If not us, then who? If not now, then when?"

If the current, and I suspect long-term, trend is to embrace "uncomfortable interpretation" as a profession, there must be ways to sustain ourselves. NAI executive director Paul Caputo, in a 2022 *Legacy* column titled "There's No

Looking Back," notes that the world "has changed considerably in the last few years" and that NAI can offer "a real live movement, creating connections to nature during a climate crisis, facilitating understanding of our past at a time when lessons from our history are of critical importance, and building bridges . . . when we feel sometimes hopelessly divided."

NAI president Parker McMullen Bushman concurs in a 2024 *Legacy* article titled "Beyond Comfort Zones: Navigating Uncomfortable Interpretation," stating that interpreters face certain "demands confronting uncomfortable truths." She writes, "As the keepers of stories and histories, interpreters have a duty to paint a full and unvarnished picture of the past and present. But presenting this picture isn't easy."

On the one hand, interpreters are fortunate to have work that is important, that can make a difference, and that provides meaning in their lives and the lives of others. On the other hand, especially when addressing uncomfortable topics, interpreters can become immersed in the story and pick up that emotional burden. This can be magnified when one's work is to connect with the broad public in potentially emotionally charged ways.

Tom Moffatt and Lynn Cartmell, in their 2021 "Leading Questions" column in *Legacy*, note, "there is ample evidence that the very nature of the work interpreters do makes them susceptible to stress-induced burnout." These authors discuss burnout in the context of exhaustion that comes from prolonged stress and that results in a sense of futility. They point out that although self-care mechanisms are important, it's also critical to have a workplace that is supportive and understanding. Therefore, strategies to support the individual interpreter over the long term can be as important as knowing how to properly organize a program or design a new exhibit.

AN INTRODUCTION TO THE STORIES

All this background, then, leads us to this book: *Inspiration for Interpreters: Moving Beyond the Treeline and Other Stories.* Most of my previous contributions to the profession have focused on providing resources to inspire excellence in the field and to advance the profession. This book is different in approach but shares that same intent. And what better way to convey the message—for those who have a passion for interpretation—than through stories?

The essays in this book focus on how we can sustain ourselves given a professional trend toward engagement with uncomfortable interpretation. The stories were chosen to help guide a shift toward a "real live movement," as Paul Caputo noted, "committed to being a force for good, and there's no looking back." The stories that follow, each in their own way, shed light on the complexities of where we find ourselves in this moment of increasingly challenging circumstances.

I will point out, at this juncture, that I have employed, to the best of my ability, various aspects of effective interpretation in the stories that follow. As with other interpreters across the globe, I strive to employ Sam Ham's TORE (theme, organized, relevant, and enjoyable) framework in which interpretation is designed strategically with a theme, is organized, is relevant, and is enjoyable. Even when writing about difficult and sometimes dark topics, I always attempt to end on a hopeful note.

I also employ the various principles first generated by Enos Mills and Freeman Tilden in their attempts to relate the material to the audience, reveal deeper meanings, and provide provocation to think more deeply about something or do something differently. I strive to feature those "gifts" that I wrote about with Ted Cable, including the gift of relationship, the gift of beauty, the gift of passion, and the gift of hope, among others.

Finally, I try to showcase universal principles that I first learned about from National Park Service leader David Larsen at the 2000 NAI national conference in Tucson, Arizona. Universal concepts—those things that just about everyone can relate to—may include opposites such as contemplation and action, solitude and community, work and leisure, victory and defeat, good and evil, life and death. Other universal concepts I employ include freedom, patriotism, companionship, suffering, justice, responsibility, kindness, courage, joy, and love.

I encourage readers to look through these chapters through the lens of effective interpretation. But more than that, I hope readers will find something in these stories that resonates with their own thoughts, feelings, aspirations, and emotions. As the author Barry Lopez once explained to me, his readers often report that although he was writing about Subject A, they were inspired to think about Subject B. In other words, readers will get out of these stories what they will.

MOVING BEYOND THE TREELINE

The longer title essay, "Moving Beyond the Treeline," now includes reference to relatively recent events focusing on those people who first lived on the land. The story further traces the trajectory of human history to include early explorers, the voyageurs, and a married couple who settled on the land, far removed from civilization. The story highlights some of the natural history of the far north and the wonder that experiences in remote nature bring to our lives.

Perhaps most important is the invitation the story offers to seek adventure in one's own life. If interpreters are to tackle an honest telling of our history to include those who have been marginalized, and if we are to share what science tells us about our relationship with the environment, then we must have outlets to inspire us and keep us going. The magic of adventure generates energy to do our best work.

I can think of few things greater to invigorate oneself than immersion in a remote landscape or similar adventure of the body, mind, and spirit. Perhaps this story will provide encouragement to pursue one's own journey of discovery. Indeed, the title of the story has a double meaning. On the one hand, it is about physical travel so far north that trees can't grow there. On the other hand, it is about moving beyond what we are familiar with and crossing boundaries.

AND OTHER STORIES

What follows next is a series of recent essays that first appeared in *Legacy* magazine as feature articles that met the theme of a particular issue. These essays were not part of my "Justice for All" column. In concert with the themes of each of the issues—such as "Interpreting Reality," "Interpreting Democracy," and "Interpreting Hope"—these additional stories collectively illuminate some of the challenges that interpreters face and some potential solutions.

The first of these essays focuses on a person I consider a mentor even though I only spent time with him over three days. Barry Lopez was a prolific author and I've read just about everything he has written. After his death on Christmas Day in 2020, I wrote a tribute about him in a themed issue of *Legacy* focused on "Interpreting Leadership." The title of that piece is "Barry Lopez: Leading by Story." Perhaps better than anyone, Lopez demonstrated through his writing the power of a story. One of the most influential things I learned from Lopez was his willingness to reveal something personal about himself that often resonated with my own experience.

This insight I gained from Lopez is apparent in the next essay, which is titled "Running for Our Lives," that appeared in a themed *Legacy* issue on "Interpreting Medicine." Here I share a personal story about a cancer diagnosis and the importance of raising funds for medical research to find cures.

I asked my dear friend and colleague Dan Dustin to review the article for me (we often share our articles with each other). After reading the essay, Dan wondered whether I should provide the main lesson—the purpose of the story, the intended message—or let readers determine that on their own. We brainstormed the possibilities. Perhaps the most obvious message is that being in the outdoors contributes to our physical, mental, and spiritual health. Physical activity in nature is like "medicine" and brings beauty, comfort, peace, inspiration, wonder, and joy into our lives. But could there be more? Here is what we came up with:

Courage—the indomitable spirit of people faced with catastrophic circumstances.
Tenacity—strength and perseverance in the face of terrible odds.

Commitment—living the lives we have to the fullest because you never know how long you have on this planet.

Gratitude—we should count our blessings.

Selflessness—one way to deal with a difficult situation is by turning outward and helping others.

The question here was whether to share the moral of the story, of which there seemed to be many. So I asked *Legacy* editor (at that time) Paul Caputo for his input. After some deliberation, Paul suggested we let the readers determine this on their own. But, he continued, "Maybe the point is to enjoy every moment." I mention this story-within-a-story because it shows, as Barry Lopez suggested to me long ago, that what someone gains from a story will vary according to the individual who hears the story. In my writing about Subject A, you might be inclined to consider Subject B. Just as with the audiences you interpret for, who, too, are sovereign.

The next essay is the only one in this collection that I coauthored, in this case with Dan Dustin. This was for a themed issue of *Legacy* on "Interpreting Reality." This problem has become increasingly important as we see the damage done by advancing false information. The title of the essay sums up our content succinctly: "Reality Matters." Dan and I grounded this piece with reference to a poem by William Butler Yeats. We address a shift, especially within just the past few years, as we observe increasingly outlandish disinformation, politically motivated lies, and conspiracy theories. Dan and I discussed what is at stake for interpreters who are committed to historic accuracy and scientific integrity, with suggestions for countering disinformation effectively and compassionately.

Related to the "Reality Matters" essay is one that appeared in the themed issue, "Interpreting Democracy." Here I refer to the life of Elijah Cummings, a Black member of the House of Representatives for more than twenty years. I paraphrase his words, asking, "When we're dancing with the angels, the question will be asked [in 2020 and every year beyond], what did we do to make sure we kept our democracy intact? Did we stand on the sidelines and say nothing?" The title of that piece is "Keeping Our Democracy Intact" and note that it was written prior to the January 6, 2021, insurrection at the US Capitol Building and couldn't be more pertinent today.

The essay that follows appeared in a themed issue on "Interpreting the Urban Landscape." My article focused on the events of 9/11, and the interpretation of the site where some of the attacks occurred, the National September 11 Memorial and Museum. I titled this piece, "Interpreting New York City's Missing Towers." The article was published in 2019 prior to the twentieth remembrance of the 9/11 terrorist attacks, at which time it was listed by Trip Advisor as the #1 museum in North America. My article is an "interpretation" of this remarkable site. I encourage all interpreters to visit.

Among many other potential personal reflections, I'd also suggest that you dwell on the shift that has taken place from a nation that truly came together after this tragic event, and where we are as a deeply divided nation today.

The last essay is titled the same as the themed *Legacy* issue, "Interpreting Hope." I begin that essay by reflecting realistically on the current situation to include climate heating events and political extremism. But I move on to consider what "hope" means and what entails a "hopeful story." The essay concludes that interpreters can change the world.

A few months ago, I visited the Museum of Tolerance in Los Angeles. As you embark on the stories in this book, I leave you with the message I found on a t-shirt I bought at the gift store: "Change the way you see the world and your role in it."

Part I

Moving Beyond the Treeline

Prologue

At the time of our subarctic canoe expedition, many years ago, this region of the Northwest Territories had not yet been designated a Canadian park and protected area but was a vast expanse of stunted boreal forest and tundra that few people had ever heard of. Now, much of the area that we traveled through—the eastern arm of Great Slave Lake, and surrounding region—has been designated the 6.5-million-acre Thaidene Nëné National Park Reserve. The park was established through the partnership of Parks Canada and Indigenous governments of the Northwest Territories. In the Denesoline (Chipewyan) language, Thaidene Nëné translates, appropriately, as "Land of the Ancestors."

At the time, I wasn't much aware of the Indigenous history of the area. Information I found through library searches was written by the early explorers to this region or was about the voyageurs who traveled by canoe, north along waterways, to trade with Indigenous peoples for furs.

The area we traveled through was first proposed as a national park in the 1960s. One of the most significant challenges to formal protection was First Nation resistance because of North American history of colonization and postcolonial land management. As in the United States, Canada confined Indigenous peoples to reservations, placed their children in boarding schools, and tried to force assimilation. Initially, First Nation peoples were opposed to national park proposals that could mean removal from ancestral territories and limitations on traditional subsistence fishing, hunting, gathering, and the practice of cultural ceremonies.

Then, in the 1990s, the mineral-rich landscape became of interest to mining companies that would exploit the area. At this point the Dene (meaning "the people") First Nation recognized the damage that would occur to the land, the water, the animals—and their way of life—if development proceeded. They chose to work collaboratively—over decades—with national and territorial governments to forge a new vision for this undervalued ecosystem that would champion respect for ancestral lands, embrace traditional ways of life, and allow for cooperative management.

Negotiations took place amid a movement that had begun to realize Canadian responsibilities to Indigenous peoples who have a spiritual, reciprocal relationship with the land. In 2019, the area was designated an Indigenous Protected Area made up of a National Park Reserve, Territorial Protected Area, and Wildlife Conservation Area. The eastern arm of Great Slave Lake, and the surrounding region, became the 6.5-million-acre Thaidene Nëné National Park Reserve.

Dene First Nation peoples can hunt, fish, trap, gather plants, and access traditional spiritual areas and burial grounds. In addition, they cooperatively manage the reserve because Indigenous peoples, with their deep firsthand understandings, have stewarded their lands and waters since time immemorial. Thaidene Nëné National Park Reserve also serves as a protected area for wildlife conservation, biological diversity, and critical habitat for caribou, bears, lynx, wolves, muskoxen, and many other key species of the far north.

Importantly, I think, in 2022 the *New York Times* Travel Desk offered a "Special Section" of the newspaper called "52 Places for a Changed World." Traditionally, the *Times* focused on "52 Places to Travel" to launch each new year by identifying new hotels and restaurants, or state-of-the-art entertainment venues.

But in 2022 the editorial staff shifted emphasis recognizing that travel is adapting to vast changes including overtourism, interpreting social and environmental justice issues, coping with climate change, and adjusting to a global pandemic. The intent was to highlight some places where tourists can be "part of the solution." The *Times* reported on fifty-two destinations (one for each week of the year) that are tackling issues such as protecting critical wild lands and threatened species, acknowledging historical wrongs, and identifying fragile communities that are preserving traditional culture.

One of the "52 Places for a Changed World" is Thaidene Nëné National Park Reserve. The listing noted that this site sets a new precedent in including Indigenous peoples in park management and oversight. Also noteworthy is that economic opportunities through sustainable tourism flow back to Dene First Nation communities. Guided experiences include fishing trips and canoe expeditions in the summer, dog sledding and observing the aurora borealis in winter, and observing subarctic wildlife year around, while also providing firsthand interpretation through cultural heritage tours. In other words, Dene First Nation peoples who live in the area are responsible for protecting, monitoring, and providing interpretation at the new park reserve.

In addition, the Dene First Nation created a "Watchers of the Land" program that provides younger generations with cultural and ecological knowledge from their elders. The Dene First Nation rangers help manage the land and pass on valuable skills to their youth.

Currently, there are many changes taking place throughout the Northwest Territories, including renaming efforts. Concern has been expressed by

Indigenous peoples who would like the name of Great Slave Lake to revert to a traditional name. The history behind the name of the lake is complex. As of now, work is well under way to change the name of Great Slave Lake through consultations with Indigenous governments.

The Thaidene Nëné National Park Reserve is one of many examples of how the story of the North American continent is being renamed, reinterpreted, and retold. The "Land of the Ancestors" can be a model of Indigenous people claiming their rightful place to inhabit their ancestral lands for physical and cultural sustenance, to assist in the management of those lands and waters, to mentor their youth to sustain cultural practices, and to be the ones who share monumental recreational activities and interpretive experiences with park visitors.

1

Voyageurs

No roads lead to Dave Olesen's place. He lives in a cabin along the north shore of Great Slave Lake, deep in the wilderness of Canada's Northwest Territories. Great Slave Lake is among the ten largest freshwater lakes in the world. It is 300 miles long and up to 140 miles wide, with a depth of more than 2,000 feet. The lake is so remote that it was not completely surveyed until the early 1920s. The surrounding landscape is mostly flat, spangled with other lakes, large and small. Stunted black spruce forest gives way to treeless tundra farther north. Here is one of North America's last great refuges for wildlife: tireless wolves and lumbering grizzlies, ungainly moose and sparring caribou, bald eagles and wailing loons.

I am a member of a group of canoeists consisting of twelve men and two women. From the community of Yellowknife to the west, we have paddled 210 miles to Olesen's cabin. Although fully versed in the mechanics of backcountry travel in canoes, we are anything but an athletic and youthful crew. Ranging in age from mid-thirties to early sixties, we have worked hard to get here.

We are delivering three handcrafted cedar-strip canoes. Olesen is hoping to establish a supplemental income during the summer months as a wilderness outfitter and canoe guide in the "barrenlands" of Canada. Just north of his cabin, about seventy miles, is the northern limit of trees and our final destination with the canoes.

As suggested by their price ($2,500 apiece), these are not ordinary canoes. They were built by members of the Minnesota Canoe Association over the course of a year. Many in our group were involved in crafting the canoes and have a due interest in paddling the finished products. Each canoe is 24 1/2 feet from bow to stern, specifically designed for long expeditions on vast lakes.

On the water, laden with four or five paddlers and three weeks of supplies, the canoes are stable and seaworthy. Moreover, the artisanship of each craft is striking. The cedar strips mesh like the narrow slats of a fine, polished hardwood floor.

This trip was planned by coleaders Leo McAvoy and Al Gustaveson. Leo is a university professor, and Al is a carpenter, under whose direction the canoes were built. The remaining crew consisted of avid canoeists with a diverse range of vocations, most all from Minnesota, the land of ten thousand lakes.

I took flights to our starting point in Yellowknife, via Edmonton, from San Diego. The rest of the group drove from Minneapolis in a crowded van. They hauled the gear and canoes in a trailer. With a rotation of drivers, they were northbound for fifty-six hours, traveling nonstop except for gasoline and meals, churning up road dust over unpaved highways.

Sigurd Olson, one of America's eloquent interpreters of wilderness, wrote in *The Lonely Land*: "There are few places left on the North American continent where [you] can still see the country as it was before Europeans came . . . but in the Canadian Northwest it can still be done."

Our adventure is reminiscent of the journeys of early explorers and voyageurs (a French word meaning "travelers") who paddled northern lakes in the heyday of the fur trade from the mid-1500s to the early 1800s. Jacques Cartier explored the St. Lawrence River, what he believed to be the Northwest Passage, in 1535. Although he didn't find the elusive passage, he traded with the Indigenous peoples, who were eager to barter for iron kettles, knives, hatchets, wool cloth, and other manufactured goods.

The Indigenous peoples traditionally cooked by dropping hot stones from a fire into clay vessels or tightly woven baskets. Imagine the convenience of using a metal pot over an open flame. Or using a steel-bladed knife to skin an animal, or an axe to fell a tree, rather than stone implements. In exchange for these luxuries, the Indigenous peoples offered, among other things, beaver pelts that were hailed back in Europe as an ideal felt for making hats. The fur enterprise continued to expand to the north and west as hunting and trapping depleted nearby beaver—and fox, lynx, wolverine, river otter, and wolf. A tremendous impact on Indigenous culture and traditions, as well as on the animals that lived there, ensued.

Grace Lee Nute wrote *The Voyageur* (1931) and *The Voyageur's Highway* (1941), long considered seminal works. Transportation along the "voyageur's highway"—an intricate system of lakes and rivers—was straightforward. Like American settlers moving west in covered wagons, the voyageurs paddled north in canoes over established routes.

According to Nute, the canoes were made from forest materials. Birch bark, fitted over a frame of cedar boards, was sewn together with the root of a conifer (often red spruce) and caulked with the melted gum from pine trees. Canoes varied in size from the enormous "Montreal" canoe (thirty-five to forty feet) that hauled five tons to the "North" canoe (twenty-five feet) that could carry one-and-a-half tons.

The vessels were well cared for. Voyageurs were careful not to run their boats into shore or paddle in high winds. An oilcloth was carried for covering the freight and on occasion for raising a sail. Large sponges were used for bailing.

Voyageurs considered themselves fortunate to engage in physical, outdoor work. The hardships of the business were dismissed; rarely did voyageurs complain. They boasted about their feats of strength and often tried to outperform each other.

Because of the tenor of their work, voyageurs fulfilled two criteria for hire. They had to be short, on average five and a half feet, so their legs could fit comfortably in a canoe without taking up precious cargo space. Furthermore, they needed strong arms and shoulders to propel the canoe and carry goods overland between lakes or around rapids. Periodic obstacles to clear and open paddling required hauling (portaging) the canoes and gear.

Freight was packaged in ninety-pound sacks. A tumpline (a strap across the forehead and attached to the load) was used to ease the burden. According to Nute, the standard load was two sacks and voyageurs occasionally carried more. Twisted ankles and bruised feet were common, and injuries from falls under enormous loads killed some voyageurs. Only drowning in dangerous rapids claimed more lives.

Nute noted that during the long light of the summer months, voyageurs spent upward of fifteen hours per day transporting their goods over land and water. A sense of urgency tended to pervade the enterprise. On the water, voyageurs took some forty strokes per minute, in unison except the steersman, to average about five miles per hour. At portages, the canoes were quickly unloaded. Then the men took off at a trot under heavy loads. Over long portages, the canoes and gear were carried perhaps a half-mile at a time. Once the full load was gathered, it was moved another half-mile. It took several trips back and forth to move the entire load. Upon reaching navigable water, canoes were reloaded and launched again.

Voyageurs took breaks on the water periodically to rest tired arms and shoulders. Pipes were lit and stories told. Voyageurs rested for as long as it took for a pipe; once the smoke cleared, it was time to move on. To pass time on the water, voyageurs burst out singing.

At camp, a typical meal was a thick soup of peas, strips of pork, and biscuits all mixed in a large pot that hung over the fire. According to Nute, etiquette varied. In some instances, the canoemen all sat around the kettle taking spoonfuls at a rapid-fire pace. Sometimes dishes were used. In other cases, the whole meal was poured out on flat rocks (to cool faster) and the voyageurs lapped it up like dogs. Afterward, pipes were lit. Around the campfire, they told exaggerated stories in which, inevitably, the storyteller was the hero.

Carolyn Podruchny provided a more recent portrait of the voyageur's life in *Making the Voyageur World* (2006), which began as a doctoral dissertation written at the University of Toronto. She offers a deeper analysis of these men and explains "they were all men" beyond the "merry workhorse" stereotypes generally portrayed in the literature or popular culture.

Podruchny noted that French Canadian voyageurs were indentured servants. They generally came from farming families who needed the money at the same time the fur trade needed labor to transport furs and goods along northern waterways. Recruiting agents would arrange contracts, or "engagements," for work during the summer months or sometimes year 'round, generally for a few years' time.

Many were attracted to the adventure of working in the fur trade. They navigated remote landscapes and new social spaces as they interacted with Indigenous cultures. At the peak of the fur trade approximately three thousand men transported furs and goods between Montreal and places far to the north and west.

Voyageurs were mostly illiterate, and they left scant written record. They expressed themselves through oral means, systems of knowledge in common with the Indigenous peoples they met. In other words, they told stories.

Perhaps one of the best-known descriptions of a voyageur's life is found in a book by Alexander Ross titled *Fur Hunters of the Far West*, published in 1855. An older voyageur related a summary of his life in the fur trade that Ross transcribed as accurately as possible. Both Nute and Podruchny quote the elder voyageur's testimony:

"'I could carry, paddle, walk and sing with any man I ever saw. . . . No portage was ever too long for me. I wanted for nothing. . . . Were I young again, I should glory in commencing the same career again. . . . There is no life so happy as a voyageur's life; none so independent; no place where a man enjoys so much variety and freedom.'"

The paradox of this happy life is that it revolved around hardship and danger. Voyageurs experienced the rewards of an outdoor lifestyle—a joyous state that comes from exercise, fresh air, comradeship, simplicity, and freedom. They were blessed with timeless days on the water, in full song, amid a backdrop of exhilarating beauty. Yet this was complemented by depravation and exposure to those same natural elements that could kill them. These seemingly contradictory forces contributed to an exuberant lifestyle that wasn't, perhaps, otherwise possible. Their highs were appreciated more because they also withstood the lows and understood the risks associated with what they were doing.

They lived on the edge.

2

Paddling

Like the voyageurs, we are delivering goods—in this instance, the canoes. Like the voyageurs, our labors are physically demanding. Like our counterparts from the past, we have a routine. And like the voyageurs, we are traveling through a landscape where nature's rhythms dominate. Unlike the voyageurs, we have volunteered our efforts. Most of us had figured this might be fun.

Wakeup call is at 5:00 in the morning. By no later than 6:30 or so, we have loaded and launched the canoes, having broken camp, and eaten a breakfast of cereal, usually, and coffee. We take short rests on the water every hour or so, the canoes huddled together for variable periods of time.

We usually cover twelve to fourteen miles before stopping for lunch. As we are weary by midday, lunch is followed by a short nap. We sprawl out almost anywhere and sleep for a half hour. Our progress is less remarkable in the afternoon as we continue to wear down. By evening, we make camp: pitch tents, gather wood, build a fire, fetch water, prepare dinner, clean up, fall asleep.

On camping ventures, I prefer to sleep out, under a sky of stars, rather than within the confines of a tent. Here we bed down in tents out of necessity. The climate in the Northwest Territories is variable. We will endure many nights—and days—of rain. This is also the time of year when mosquitoes and blackflies flourish. (The mosquito netting on the tents is designed to keep insects out.) Finally, there are no stars to look at, even given a cloudless sky, because it does not get dark this far north in July. One member of the group became the subject of well-deserved ridicule when he admitted he brought a flashlight.

It is our first evening on Great Slave Lake, and I wish I had known to bring my own tent. We have seven tents and sleep in twosomes. Like most of the tents here, mine is sturdy and will sleep three or four; for two it is spacious. The tent I now share is, by a considerable margin, the smallest here. It sleeps two bulgingly. For lack of space, one person enters and gets settled, then the other. Over the course of the journey, this tent will leak rain through the sides. Mosquitoes and blackflies will mysteriously enter through the fabric at night. The very last evening the center pole will snap, and the tent will collapse entirely in the midst of gale winds and heavy rain.

At the moment, my dismay is focused on the actions of my newly acquainted tentmate. His name is Dan. He is large, strong. Dan has discovered, this first day of our journey, that his boots leak. As I enter the tent, having sat a short distance away enjoying the rich light of late evening, I see that he has just finished patching his boots with rubber cement. Surrounded by boundless terrain he has chosen, to my astonishment, the inside of our shelter for his task. It is too late to suggest another plan; the tent is rank with glue fumes. This first night, I have strange, glue-inspired dreams and wake up with a headache and sore throat.

~

The second day finds us still seeking the optimal arrangement of crew so that the boats are evenly manned. The canoes have four paddling stations: two in front and two in back. There is room for one paddler in the far front of the bow, and just behind there is sufficient space for two paddlers, side by side. Likewise, there is one paddler in the stern, the captain, and space for two paddlers just forward. In the mid-ship of each canoe is storage space for our gear.

We have concluded, so far, that one canoe will bear the four largest men, each in a paddling station, one behind the other. With some experimentation, we have also determined that the other canoes will have three small paddlers up front and the remaining two in back, one behind the other.

I occupy the position in front of the stern in a canoe of five. Behind me is Tom, tall and lean, in a red wool shirt, cleaving the water with long, powerful strokes.

Tom tells me he has been married almost twenty years. He and his wife have created a lifestyle that celebrates the past. Together they researched, obtained plans, and built an eighteenth-century Cape Cod house on their sixty-acre property in Independence, Minnesota.

Tom makes his own syrup from the maple trees on his land. His wife plants "antique" flowers in their garden; that is, flowers that were commonly grown when America was first settled by Europeans. Another of their pastimes is putting together "antique" meals. Elaborate menus were recorded back in the 1700s, and through diligent efforts, Tom and his wife have duplicated a George Washington Christmas dinner. Cooked in the traditional manner, this feast offers a half-dozen main courses and just as many desserts.

The meals planned for this trip are hearty and substantial, although otherwise no relation to Tom's banquets. For dinner we have "one-pot" meals. Spaghetti. Linguini. Macaroni. Other nights, we eat chili or stew with cornbread or biscuits. The baking is conducted "dutch oven style," using coals above and below a covered pan for uniform heat. Fresh-caught lake trout, northern pike, and arctic grayling supplement the planned menu. The critical factor—and this can't be overstated—is that there is plenty of food. We eat like voyageurs.

There is always a pot of coffee and something for dessert. Brownies or cheesecake. Gingerbread or mousse pudding. Our first night out, we ate two Jack Daniels pecan pies, baked and given to us by one of Olesen's friends in Yellowknife, to christen the journey.

Tom and I continue to talk as we ply open water. The members of this canoe have made several shifts of position from yesterday's arrangement, and there is a considerable difference in our performance today. Everything has come together, and our group is paddling as one. In full synchronization, we are cutting swiftly through the water. The momentum of the canoe is bracing as we move through the cool morning breeze.

Indeed, we are outpacing the others. Looking back, we see that they have fallen far behind. We stop to let them catch up. They are lagging again shortly. Once more we stop. It is obvious, now, that our canoe team is stronger. The other paddlers are killing themselves trying to keep up. There must be an exchange of personnel, for balance.

I find myself in the same position in another canoe. Now Leo is behind me. Leo is a solid outdoorsman—compact, sturdy. He is soft-spoken with dark, graying hair and beard. He was an officer in the Navy.

Leo is a professor at the University of Minnesota. He pushes students under his charge, though in a benevolent manner, and not beyond their capabilities. It is a delicate balance, and he will employ the very same ingenuity in motivating this group to reach its destination. Leo takes this assignment seriously. Dave Olesen wants the canoes delivered north of his cabin to Maufelly Bay on Walmsley Lake. Leo said we could do it, and he intends to see that it happens. Leo understands the variables that may delay us, so he constantly pushes forward.

The coleader of the trip, Al, is Leo's lighthearted foil. Al is buoyant and playful. His beard is full and gray, his crown balding. He is a diminutive man, gnome-like, full of songs, tales, and laughter. He speaks convincingly on most any subject. He is sinewy and strong. In proper garb, a few hundred years ago, he would offer the personality, stamina, and size to have passed for a voyageur.

We paddle on, passing through clusters of small islands, eventually stopping on one to eat. Lunch is mostly an assemblage of high-energy food: peanut butter and jam on biscuits, crackers and cheese, dried fruit and nuts, cookies, and hard candy. As we eat, we are scolded by arctic terns. They scream at us, swooping menacingly from above. They are protecting their nests that are on the ground and contain three or four mottled, dark green eggs. The eggs are well camouflaged in the rocky tundra; so much so that one is accidentally stepped on.

We have been drawn here, most of us, out of wonder and respect for the landscape and its wildlife. That deference seems compromised as we paddle away from the island, leaving behind a crushed egg and the hysterical cries of the terns. The sky is gray when we land for the night, and we eat our dinner through a drizzle. I drift to sleep to the patter of rain on the tent.

~

We break camp and launch the canoes in an early morning shower. The rain is not hard enough to keep the mosquitoes down. My arms and shoulders are sore, and my legs cramped, as are everyone's, as we break into the cadence of paddling. Al notes, in reference to the tight quarters of the canoes and our physical labor, "What hurts is everything between my neck and my toes."

A cloud of mosquitoes follows each canoe as we leave the mainland. Paddling in the cold rain, enduring the infernal mosquitoes, I reflect there are only nineteen days to go. Mosquitoes are as much a parcel of the north as the wolves and caribou, the unnamed lakes, the steel cold winters, the northern lights. The Indigenous peoples of this land, the early adventurers, and all those who have followed suffer the presence of these winged pests.

In 1833, George Back launched the first exploration into the barrenlands, seeking the mouth of the Great Fish River. He wrote in his journal: "There is certainly no form of wretchedness, among those to which the chequered life of a voyageur is exposed, at once so great and humiliating as the torture inflicted by these puny blood-suckers." He added, "They convey[ed] to us the moral lesson of man's helplessness; since with all our boasted strength and skill, we were unable to repel these feeble atoms of the creation."

In 1907, Ernest Thompson Seton set off on a voyage to study caribou and other aspects of the natural history of "the arctic prairies." He devoted an entire chapter of his subsequent book to mosquitoes. Seton liked to document hard numbers. He devised, of all things, a "mosquito gauge," in which he held up his bare hand for five seconds and then counted the number of mosquitoes on the back side. Although crude, his method did provide a relative measure of the abundance of mosquitoes. He found that the concentration at the start of his journey, in Saskatchewan, was mild, in the range of five to ten mosquitoes, compared with that further north. On Great Slave Lake, in July, the numbers reached fifty to sixty. Seton wrote, "It was possible to number them only by killing them and counting the corpses." Still further north, in the barrenlands, the hand test revealed 100 to 125 mosquitoes.

Seton also calculated the number of mosquitoes on his tent. He registered thirty mosquitoes on six square inches of the fabric and as the tent was uniformly covered, came up with twenty-four thousand mosquitoes over the entire surface. At one point, Seton counted "a round 400 mosquitoes" boring away on the jacket of the comrade paddling in front of him.

To ward off mosquitoes and blackflies, we carry plenty of insect repellant. We have loosely woven string jackets, soaked in repellant, that we wear over our clothes. We have fine mesh headnets to cover our faces and necks. And still the infuriating pests hover and penetrate. With no inclination to tally the number of mosquitoes on the backs of those in front of me, my imagination wanders as we slog on.

We reach mile sixty of our journey by the end of the day. We unload the canoes in a light shower. The rocks are slippery, and several people take hard falls. Then the skies begin to clear. There will be a little free time before we prepare dinner, so I piece together my fishing rod, attach a bright lure, and promptly land three arctic grayling. The fish are filleted, along with some lake trout that someone else caught.

We place the filets in a plastic bag, then in a large pot that is sunk just offshore with a rock on top. This way we do not needlessly attract wildlife, like bears, and the lake refrigerates the fish. The water is biting cold—indeed, there are still a few ice floes on the water in July, a reminder that the surface is frozen throughout the winter.

~

The next day we have fish and potatoes for breakfast before breaking camp, then paddle the canoes through a thick, early morning mist. The air is moist and cool. Piercing the shroud of mist, the sun punches through fingers of light, which radiate from the sky like the spokes of a wheel. An old friend once told me that this is called the "God effect." The divine rays brush the water.

The lake is calm as the fog vanishes. The water is as smooth and as reflective as a mirror. It is as if we are paddling in animation through clouds floating above and drifting below us.

The calm morning becomes increasingly breezy, and we are windbound by afternoon. Most of the crew gathers near the canoes. I hike up a hill to a vantage point, a nook in the rocks. I can see the flotilla of canoes far below. Starbursts of sunlight sparkle on the waves in Hearne Channel. A long, narrow island—Blanchette Island—forms the channel. There are delicate puffs of clouds in the pale blue sky. Closer, birch leaves flutter in the wind. The cool breeze is refreshing in the intense, powerful rays of the sun.

As the wind subsides, late in the afternoon, we paddle onward. Just before landing for the night, we see two bald eagles high in the trees on McKinley Point. Their head and tail feathers catch the serene evening light. The eagles fly from one perch to another, but not away from us, as we drift silently in awe.

Our response to the wildlife contrasts with that of the early explorers here. In George Back's journal, he recounted sighting a "majestic fishing eagle" seated in a tree. His men flagrantly shouted at the eagle to frighten and flush it. I can imagine the scene, the men carrying on like stooges, the product of a different time, a different mentality. As Back reported, the eagle "unscared by our cries, reigned in solitary state, the monarch of the rocky wilderness."

It is time to find a camp. The terrain is rugged, and it takes some scouting to locate a suitable site.

~

On the fifth day, we paddle twenty-three miles, following our now well-established routine. After dinner, we gather for a camp meeting. Leo seems pleased with our progress so far. In five days we have covered 103 miles. We are almost halfway to Olesen's cabin. It is good fortune that the wind has not held us back any more than it has. Leo reads us an excerpt from George Back's journal. Then Al breaks out a worn copy of *The Collected Poems of Robert Service*. He reads "The Lure of Little Voices," an excerpt of which follows, that sums up why so many of us are here:

Yes, they're wanting me, they're haunting me, the awful lonely places;
They're whining and they're whimpering as if each had a soul;
They're calling from the wilderness, the vast and God-like spaces,
The stark and sullen solitudes that sentinel the Pole . . .
It's the lure of little voices, it's the mandate of the Wild.

I spent a summer in Alaska many years ago working at Denali National Park and Preserve. A few verses from Service's "The Spell of the Yukon" sum up that experience and why I was so eager to return to the subarctic.

The summer—no sweeter was ever; The sunshiny woods all athrill;
The grayling aleap in the river, The bighorn asleep on the hill.
The strong life that never knows harness; The wilds where the caribou call;
The freshness, the freedom, the farness— Oh God! how I'm stuck on it all . . .
There's a land where the mountains are nameless,
And the rivers all run God knows where;
There are lives that are erring and aimless, And deaths that just hang by a hair;
There are hardships that nobody reckons; There are valleys unpeopled and still;
There's a land—oh, it beckons and beckons, And I want to go back and I will . . .

Such is the magic—the lure—of the far north.

~

Sunday is, sort of, a day of rest. We paddle fifteen miles before stopping for lunch, then set camp on an island. With the afternoon for leisure, I take a dip in the lake, lathering and rinsing afterward with a large pot of water on land. Then

I launder my clothes, again on shore, and set them on rocks to dry. Refreshed, I assemble my pole and fish until I've caught two lake trout.

Popular wilderness sites show wear from an onslaught of recreational use. On this trip, we follow "leave no trace" strategies to protect the pristine environment. Although we are far removed from civilization and relatively few others travel here, out of habit and respect we minimize our impact.

Bathing, laundering clothes, or washing dishes with soap can suds up a lake or stream. This not only affects the aquatic ecology, it provides evidence that others have traveled through. So we wash away from the water source and use biodegradable soap. Likewise, we keep our fires small and collect only fallen, dead wood. This practice helps conserve dwindling wood supplies.

~

Well rested, we paddle twenty-seven miles, to mile 145, over the course of a clear day with cool breezes. We approach Plummer's Outpost, which is a "resort" for people who are flown in for the good fishing. We see, occasionally, motorboats carrying fishing parties. This is a different approach to experiencing the landscape.

At Plummer's, patrons sleep and dine in the rustic complex and are, therefore, more removed from the rhythms of the subarctic summer. By day, they zip around in motorboats from cove to cove using sonar devices to locate fish. Guides navigate the water for the paying customers. The landscape passes quickly as the boats dash about under the drone of outboard motors.

On a prominent rocky point, we see huge boulders covered with lichens. Carved into the spongy lichens are names and dates. This form of vandalism is representative of a different creed. It is a self-absorbed ritual, a proclamation for all to witness, "I was here."

Just past Plummer's we spot a black bear. From this point on, there is almost no presence, or evidence, of other people.

~

This morning, we paddle ten miles to the Mountain River. George Back, in his early exploration, vividly described a prominent mountain here, yet with even the wildest use of our imaginations, we never see it. The wind picks up, and we are once again windbound for the afternoon.

Snow in deep packs covers the ground. We explore a cabin, now in total disarray, abandoned by a miner. Sorting through the debris, I can imagine the rusticity and solitude of living here. Within this evidence of the past, history comes alive. In this cabin, I can see and touch the lifestyle of a miner long ago. Historian David McCullough noted, "We need the past for our sense of who we are . . . [and] because it is an extension of the experience of being alive."

Dan, my tentmate, fishes a pool where a river enters the lake. He makes five casts and reels in five fish. Then we move on to our camp for the night.

~

The ninth day we paddle toward a solar halo, a ring of light around the sun with faint rainbow colors. According to northern lore, this forecasts a violent shift in weather.

We stop for lunch on an island known as Bigstone Point. A red-throated loon flies over us low and menacingly. We are near her nest. We see a single, large egg at the edge of a pond. The pond sits in the middle of the island, and we are on the opposite side of the nest. I feel an ineffable sense of tension as the loon comes at us again and again.

Suddenly, our oldest member, Venice, begins violently choking. He is above everyone else, high on some boulders. Leo bounds up to him, determines he is gagging on food, and applies the Heimlich maneuver. The first abdominal thrust is ineffective. Leo is more forceful in his second attempt as Venice struggles for air, but this too fails to dislodge the food in his throat. The third thrust is a mighty, desperate attempt to save Venice. It works, and Venice can breathe again. Although he is clearly shaken up and in pain, he handles himself as if nothing has happened. I talk with him, uncomfortable with his nonchalance, as others glance nervously toward us. (Upon our return to civilization, X-rays revealed that the abdominal thrust that saved Venice's life also broke one of his ribs.)

We camp for the evening next to a large cove where several of us swim, briefly, in the shallow, frigid water. Waves from one to two feet break on the unprotected shore like the crash of ocean surf.

One member of the group has been saving something special—a bottle of brandy, a vintage from long ago, a pricey gift of appreciation he received from a business transaction that saved a company a lot of money. We drink with gratitude as the amber light of the sun reflects off the cliffs on the other side of McCleod Bay.

~

On the next day, our tenth, we arrive at Olesen's place, 210 miles from our starting point.

3

Olesen's Place

As we approach Olesen's cabin, we set off the howling of some thirty or forty dogs. Olesen is a dog musher. He breeds, trains, and races sled dogs. His work demands living on the northern skirts of civilization.

Among other long-distance races, Olesen has competed in the Iditarod Trail Sled Dog Race, the 1,100-mile Alaskan race from Anchorage to Nome, and the 350-mile John Beargrease Sled Dog Marathon along the north shore of Lake Superior in Minnesota. Unlike a human marathon, which is completed in a couple hours, the major sled dog races take several days. The winning time for the Iditarod is about a week and a half. Sled dog racing demands the endurance of the Tour de France and is similarly dominated by a few big names and a large field of lesser knowns.

On shore, we are greeted by three friendly puppies and Olesen, who heard the commotion. The puppies, energetic and playful, scamper about our legs.

Olesen invites us to look around his property. He owns but an acre of land, which is a moot point because he has no neighbors. Olesen has lived in his cabin for three years. For transportation, he has a plane, a motorboat, a canoe, and the dogs. He fishes and hunts. He can kill one moose per year and unlimited caribou. The butchered meat he keeps outside in a cache, an elevated platform for storing food, that is inaccessible to wildlife. The outside temperature is so cold that the meat stays frozen through the winter. Any day, a barge is due to deliver 10,000 pounds of dog food and 1,200 pounds of dry groceries to supplement fish and wild meat for the coming year.

Olesen is, by his own definition, thrifty. He must be. To field a competitive sled dog team is expensive. Only the top dog mushers earn much from race purses, and generous sponsorship is hard to come by. Because seasonal work is necessary for a predictable income, Olesen is buying these custom-built canoes to launch a venture called Et-Then Expeditions Ltd. He will offer "journeys of adventure and education in the far north." According to Olesen, Et-Then means "caribou" in the Chipewyan language. Much of the cultural and natural history of this region revolves around the caribou. Et-Then canoe routes and base camps will be influenced by the movements of caribou herds.

Olesen is good at cutting corners. In the days to come, I note he always wears the same work clothes. He recently let his airplane mechanic cut his hair, and it looks like it. He has traveled with his dogs by truck, by boat, by plane, and by train. Most often he is on the road in beat up pickup trucks overflowing with dogs and gear. Traveling to and from races, Olesen and his partners are inclined to drive nonstop. Camping by the side of the road in the middle of winter isn't promising, and motels are too expensive. So he and his friends just keep driving. Although Olesen may be thrifty, he isn't cheap. With all the vagaries of his line of work Olesen notes, proudly, that at present he is breaking even.

Olesen has the fortune, or the bane depending on perspective, of a physical lifestyle. His subsistence ways and upkeep of the kennel translate into hard work. He chops firewood for winter temperatures that drop below minus 40 degrees Fahrenheit. He maintains his cabin and outbuildings. He hauls food and water every day for his dogs. He uses a shovel often.

Olesen is, as much as one can be nowadays, self-sufficient. Compared to what most of us are accustomed to, his lifestyle is remarkable in its simplicity. If he needs something he cannot rush to the store.

Olesen accepts uncertainty. He answers to the rhythms of a desolate, uncompromising, yet stately land. He has a sense of place. His lifestyle keeps him strong. He is removed from the congestion, the pollution, the clamor, the frenzied pace of society as most of us know it. In the autumn, when snow has fallen and the lakes freeze, Olesen thrills in swift and silent travel behind a team of dogs.

Both art and science define Olesen's work with his dogs. Many still hold images of dog driving when large dogs, kept in line by whip and club, pulled heavy loads during the gold rush days storied in Jack London's *The Call of the Wild* and *White Fang*. Now, smaller, faster dogs are employed in racing teams, and cruelty and neglect have been replaced by affinity and care. At all major sled dog races veterinarians conduct, among other things, blood tests to check for prohibited drugs.

A strong bond exists between most mushers and their dogs. The most successful long-distance racers consider everything from dog nutrition to athletic training techniques, to obedience, to canine psychology. Olesen strives to breed dogs that are tough, fast, eager, and responsive. The puppies cavorting at our heels will make up teams of the future.

Olesen's log cabin is laid out like the letter "T." The stem serves as the living quarters with a wood-burning stove, a table, and provisions. The room that branches to the left is a study, full of books. To the right is a small bedroom.

On the other side of the cabin are plywood dog houses, spaced evenly in a sandy area. The dogs are chained and have run of a small radius around their shelters. Today the dogs are mostly sedate. By subarctic standards this sunny afternoon, maybe 72 degrees, is a sizzler.

At the far end of the dog yard is a wolf that paces incessantly. Olesen found a wolf den and took two young puppies, a male and female, from a litter of four. The male escaped. Olesen's desire is to breed the female with his dogs. He figures that one-eighth wolf could provide for certain desirable characteristics in a line of sled dogs. He also tells us that the Native Inuits are opposed to the keeping of wolves. He rationalizes keeping this wolf because so many people in the far north kill them to cash in on $400 per pelt, and keeping a live wolf, by comparison, seems reasonable.

Unlike the other dogs, which are domesticated, the wolf is clearly unhappy and behaves neurotically, like a caged animal in a zoo. Watching this one pace, its nervous energy, its longing to be free, I can't help but feel pity for the creature and a certain appreciation for the Indigenous peoples' wisdom.

After setting camp in the woods, most of us take a swim in a sandy cove. Later, several of us gather to hear Olesen share tales of his three years here working the land, taking caribou and moose, encounters with bears, a mink that got into his cabin. Then we return to our camp for the night.

~

Today we will leave Great Slave Lake. We have just a three-mile paddle before we begin portaging—carrying the canoes overland from lake to lake to our final destination, which is seventy miles to the north.

Leo follows the canoes in a small outboard boat that will serve as Olesen's transportation back to his cabin at the end of the day. I am paddling just in front of Olesen, who has taken Leo's position in the stern and is handling one of the canoes for the first time. The water is rough; the most turbulent we have paddled in. The blustery weather would have kept us ashore if not for the short distance to our first portage. As we pass close to a point of land, the waves reverberate off the rocky cliff, the turbulence pushing the canoes like a rolling sea.

Before moving to the Northwest Territories, Olesen lived in Ely, the same town in northern Minnesota that writer Sigurd Olson lived in. Of only a few select books in his cabin's bedroom are three or four by Sigurd Olson, who was instrumental in the efforts to preserve Minnesota's Boundary Waters Canoe Area Wilderness.

Olesen left Ely, a relatively quaint town to an urban observer, because of increasing commercialism and what he perceived as "trendiness" and "cliques." Likewise, he is concerned that more people are being attracted yet further north for the wrong reasons. He tells me he worries about yachts on Great Slave Lake and people coming to play golf at midnight on Ellesmere Island. He doesn't believe this land should be utilized to fill a void for those who would come expecting to be entertained.

Olesen is drawn by the remoteness and a lifestyle that is conducive to raising and training sled dogs. He is not a hermit; he enjoys company, although he suggests this would be a good place to be a hermit. Olesen, however, is married. He met his wife, Kristen, at a wedding. To bring in much needed income, Kristen is a cook at a mining camp, far away for the summer, although she is taking some time off to join us for the last few days of this journey.

4

Portaging

So dat's de reason I drink tonight To de man of de Grand Nor' Wes' For hees heart was young, an' hees heart was light So long as he's leevin' dere— I'm proud of de sam' blood in my vein I'm a son of de Nort' Win wance again— So we'll fill her up till de bottle's drain An' drink to de Voyageur.

—William Henry Drummond, 1905

Our first portage is two miles overland from Great Slave Lake to the first of a series of unnamed lakes leading us north. According to Olesen, this route to Walmsley Lake has never been done before.

Each portage requires three trips to the next lake. The first trip is an overview of the route in which we carry our personal packs (clothes, a sleeping bag, camera, fishing gear, and so on). On the second leg, we transport the canoes and assorted community gear, including food packs. The last trip, we carry a collection of leftover packs and whatever else remains, such as canoe paddles, life vests, and the wanigan—a scythe shaped wood crate that fits snugly in one canoe and contains an assemblage of awkward gear including a saw, a gas stove, pots, pans, and other cooking supplies.

To advance these two miles requires a to-and-fro total of ten miles; five times the mileage gained. This first portage will consume an entire day. For long portages, such as this, we break the labor into stages that provide more frequent "rests" as we walk back to pick up another load. We haul all the gear about a half-mile before moving on.

Carrying personal packs and food packs is relatively easy, although one member, an avid backpacker, observes that this is the first time he has ever carried a load that he can't lift himself—a food pack weighing 100 pounds. More difficult is carrying the canoes that weigh in the range of 175 pounds.

Each canoe is hoisted up and over by four or five people and set on the shoulders of two carriers. A yoke, attached to the canoes for portaging, fits on the neck and shoulders of each carrier; one person in front, one in back. Only seven of us (and Olesen) are strong enough to share the weight of a canoe for any distance, and are, therefore, almost always members of the three pairs who advance the beasts.

Leo and I are a team for this portage. We set out like oxen, heads inside the canoe that rests upside down on our shoulders. I am in the front and can see only a few yards ahead because the overturned canoe blocks most of my view. We follow someone carrying a pack who helps to direct us over the route.

The canoes, so graceful on water, are cumbersome and awkward on land. The weight bears down, focused on our shoulders, like a vise. Often the burden shifts entirely to opposite shoulders of the carriers, my left shoulder, Leo's right. Frustrated, we blame each other for a problem that turns out to be consistent among all partners.

It is not so much the weight or pain that bothers me as the fact that carrying the canoes through this terrain is dangerous. Every step must be deliberate, for to falter would be to get crushed beneath the bulk of 175 pounds of cedar. In the first stage of this portage, the footing is difficult. We walk a route that parallels a ridge, and the ground is as solid as a wet sponge. Our feet sink with every step. The second stage is even worse— through a swamp. I step high, as a moose would, over the hummocks and into the wet bog.

It is raining now, pattering on top of the canoe, and draining down the sides. The water runs down my wrists where I hold the canoe and gathers in my rain jacket at the crook of each elbow. Upon setting the canoe on the ground at the end of this stage I pour a pint of water out of each sleeve.

The next stage offers solid footing along a sandy esker, a ridge deposited by streams under glacial ice long ago. On the first trip (with a pack) of each stage, I develop a habit of noting a certain landmark along the route, toward the end, to gauge when we will be close to putting the canoes down on the second trip. For this advance, my marker is a wild rose, the fragile petals knocked to the earth by the force of rain.

A National Park Service colleague in Alaska, who became close to me as a friend, gave me a drawing she said was special to her. A line sketch of roses, the caption read: "Wild roses bring happy thoughts." As we carry the canoe past the wild rose in preparation to finally set it down—wet, weary, shoulders throbbing—these words ring true.

The next stage of the portage continues along the esker to our camp for the night. After setting camp on higher ground, we move the canoes through another swamp to the lake in which we will launch them in the morning. We eat under a tarp, protected from the rain, then retire for the evening, completely spent. Olesen, meantime, has gone all the way home to feed his dogs.

We launch the canoes in the morning and commence a series of portages from lake to lake. Olesen joins us once again. From his cabin, he took his motorboat to the portage, then hiked to our camp. He has a small canoe with him that he can carry alone, and he will return home this evening, retracing our path over land and water.

On land we follow a network of caribou trails so well traveled that in places the path is fifteen inches deep. There is evidence of caribou everywhere. Antlers, fur, and scat—millions of pellets, like black jellybeans, scattered across the landscape.

The trees are mostly alder and black spruce. Closer to the ground is Labrador tea and blueberry. Carrying the wanigan with Olesen over a short portage, he notes this will be a good year for blueberries, which he collects as they ripen at the end of the summer. Later, while portaging a canoe, he recites "The Voyageur" from a collection of poetry, *The Habitant*, by William Henry Drummond. Habitants were French settlers in Canada, many of whom became voyageurs. Leo, charmed by the verse, expresses an interest in seeing Drummond's work. (A few days later, Olesen will fly over our camp in his plane to check our progress and to drop a plastic jug into the water, full of fresh brownies and a book of Drummond's poetry for Leo.)

We face a strong headwind and whitecaps on the last lake for the day. At camp the wind is so fierce that a gust dislodges and blows away a tent (which is subsequently retrieved) that was staked into the ground. It begins to rain as we prepare dinner. Gingerbread and coffee for dessert rekindle our spirits.

After dinner I walk along the lakeshore alone in a light sprinkle. I stop to watch an arctic tern fishing. It is patrolling the length of the lake. The flight is purposeful, the strokes of the wings deep. It is hunting for small fish and insects. Several times it dives, stopping short of the water. Then, while I am standing motionless, it hits the water in an explosion directly in front of me.

~

This new day we continue to leapfrog a series of lakes. Paddle and portage. Paddle and portage. It rains intermittently all day and the winds become progressively stronger. Whitecaps begin to form on the water as we face strong headwinds. I ask Leo, an accomplished sailor, about the velocity of the wind, which he supposes is up to thirty-five knots (or about forty miles per hour). The day is cold and damp; the mood is somber. At one portage, Al, carrying the stern end of a canoe, sinks knee deep in muck and must be pulled out.

One person, who has distinguished himself as being outmatched by the conditions, feels compelled to verbalize his misery as we start yet another portage. "Now my rain pants are slipping," he complains. "What else can possibly go wrong?" The voyageurs of past centuries would have been ruthless. To the credit of several men on this trip, our complainer has been handled with kid gloves, and in retrospect he will forget the hardships. At this point in the trip, however, he is miserable.

At dinner we flip a canoe on its side and extend a tarp from it for shelter. Several people snuggle into the gut of the canoe, others scatter under the tarp near the fire. After everyone else has gone to bed, I stay up with Leo and Al and we talk wishfully of reaching the Hoarfrost River.

It is important to Leo, especially, that we get the canoes to their destination. We told Olesen that we would deliver them to Maufelly Bay on Walmsley Lake, and Leo wants to honor that. (This is also where we have arrangements for pick up by a Twin Otter plane that will land on the water and carry us back to our starting point in Yellowknife.)

~

After a windy night, Dan opens the tent flap and reports the weather. It is cold; in the forties. Cloudy. Looks like rain.

We break camp and paddle across a lake to face a long portage through thick vegetation. So we can follow the most direct route, we tie bandanas on stunted spruce trees at strategic points to guide our way. On higher ground, we build rock cairns, three rocks one atop the other, as markers. Navigating the route is still a challenge.

Having advanced our personal gear, Dan and I set out with a canoe. Our navigator loses the route, and it slowly becomes evident that we are lost. Rather than wander about aimlessly with a canoe on our shoulders, we set it down and determine our bearings. We are far off track. This is a tough portage, and the extra effort we have caused ourselves is demoralizing.

As we enter the next lake, we face our stiffest headwind yet. We paddle, making progress by the inch, until our arms feel like jelly. We come around a point and enter the next lake through a narrow channel just deep enough for the canoes. We had anticipated this being a short portage and are delighted to slip through without unloading and transporting all the gear. As we paddle to the end of the next lake, it looks as if we might be able to slip through another narrow channel, but the water is too shallow for the fully loaded canoes. Rather than portage, we hop into the frigid water to lighten the load and push the canoes through.

After paddling across another lake, we stop for lunch. Several people sack out on top of the packs. Shortly, we walk over the portage to assess the wind, which is fierce and kicking up whitecaps on the water. Waves one to two feet high are crashing on the rocky shoreline. At the head of the stream between the two lakes is a protected, calmer site where it might be possible to load and launch the canoes, one at a time.

Al dreads fighting the wind again and questions whether we can get across the lake, even assuming we can launch the canoes. Leo thinks we can do it; we've had lunch, we've rested, we're on a mission. Al walks away silently with his dissenting opinion and comes back over the portage hauling a canoe.

We set the first craft on the water for loading. Leo is in the water, immersed near to his waist, holding the canoe against the shore—otherwise it would be smashed against the rocks in the channel. All loaded, the first canoe sets out with slow but steady progress. We repeat the procedure with the second canoe. The last canoe is ours. Leo keeps the canoe steady, near the bow, as we load and get in. As Leo releases the boat, we paddle furiously to avoid being blown into the rocks, and as the canoe passes Leo, he dives into the stern. It was a tricky maneuver, and we break into a chorus of cheers as we edge out into the lake.

We next face a series of short portages. Over the shortest, Al and I team up to carry two canoes, one after the other, just to say we did it.

After the last lake, we make a half-mile portage over stable terrain to our camp. The wind is blowing hard. It is difficult carrying the canoes because they are picked up off our shoulders by the wind like unwieldy kites. Two canoes make it over to our camp; the last we leave until morning.

Our dinner this evening is one of Leo's specialties, linguini with clams. He cooks onion, garlic, and mushrooms in olive oil. This is added to a large pot of cooked and drained noodles, along with canned clams and cubed mozzarella cheese. You stir and let it sit until the cheese melts.

The entertainment for the night includes another excerpt from Back's journal, read by Leo, and William Henry Drummond's "The Voyageur," read by Al. After everyone has meandered toward bed, I walk high atop a ridge. The gray sky drizzles rain. To the south, I see the last lake we were on where, nearby, a canoe still lies. To the north is the lake we will be on tomorrow. Our camp is far below, next to a stand of trees. Our tiny village is miniscule, insignificant in this expanse of wild country. I am overwhelmed by the sheer space of the scene.

Most of our time is consumed with paddling, portaging, setting camp and breaking camp, sleeping, and eating. There is scant solitude to reflect upon where we are, the magnificence of the landscape, our distance from other humans, the wild creatures that are adapted to living here. I try to take time such as this, as often as possible, to walk away. That most of the others are content with the social aspects of the trip bewilders me. Then again, they have been friends for a long time. Or perhaps they are too tired to take strolls late at night.

Rain patters on the tent through the night until morning. My feet and shoulders hurt so much from hauling the canoes I can't sleep. Aspirin does nothing. The tent is leaking—it gets worse as the journey wears on—and seems to be getting smaller. Dan and I are becoming progressively annoyed with each other in these small, uncomfortable quarters.

~

At breakfast Dan announces that he and I will flip a coin to see which of us carries the canoe that was left behind. The loser will carry the canoe with Leo. Why this should be narrowed down to the three of us, arbitrarily, does not cross my mind at this early hour, so I don't question the plan. Someone finds a coin and flips it. I call out, "Tails never fails." The coin comes up heads and off I trudge with Leo.

Upon returning, our complainer is in rare form. "Bright morning," someone offers. "The only things bright about this morning are my yellow teeth," he replies.

Before long, we are on the water fighting a headwind and waves, from trough to crest of at least two feet. Finally, beyond a narrow spit of land is the Hoarfrost River. This portage will be our last from a lake; those we encounter next will be around the rapids of the Hoarfrost River as we paddle upstream to Walmsley Lake.

Still far from shore, where waves are crashing on a sandy beach lined with willows, my eye catches a sturdy creature bounding over the ridge toward us. It is a man, dressed completely in bright blue rain gear.

5

Aki

We know, immediately, that this is Aki, who is traveling solo in a sea kayak. He had stopped at Olesen's cabin several days before us and had been encouraged to try this new route. We knew he was ahead of us, but because of his head start, we never expected to see him. Aki explains that he has been windbound for three days here—days that we had pushed on. He helps us carry our gear over the portage, then we brew a pot of coffee.

Aki lives in Tokyo, among the world's largest and most densely populated cities, and he confirms the obvious: "Big city. Crowded." This is his fifth trip to the Canadian north. He has taken one other long vacation. Several years back, he bicycled from Los Angeles to Washington, DC, in forty-five days. He is on his way, now, to the mouth of the Coppermine River far to the north. He subsists mostly on fresh fish and either rice or instant mashed potatoes. Our group is attracted to seeing another person in such a remote area and the feeling is mutual. Aki clearly enjoys our company.

For a few minutes we are alone, and I ask Aki what draws him, again and again, to this landscape. He struggles with the question. In his broken English he says that he likes open space. "No people. No hurry." The answer, however, lies in a phrase he repeats five or six times.

"Settle down," he says.

Huge expanses of wild nature, I believe Aki is saying, lend perspective to our everyday existence. This respite gives us a fresh, firsthand look at our world—and ourselves. We come closer to the roots of our existence. Wilderness experience lends itself to a sense of freedom, stability, inner peace, gratitude, and joy.

In wilderness, we appreciate that we are rather small amid a bigger picture. Indeed, we have the opportunity to settle down. To think clearly. To breathe deeply. To push ourselves physically. To absorb our surroundings. To appreciate the forces that created the beauty before us. To luxuriate in the moment.

But now it is time for us to move on. We leave Aki, who is in no hurry, to battle the wind once again.

6

A Complete Desolation, a Northern Fairyland

But surely we carry this civilization too far, and are in danger of warping our natural instincts by too close observance of the rules that some mysterious force obliges us to follow when we herd together in big cities.... A dweller in cities is too wrapped up in the works of man to have much respect left for the works of God, and to him the loveliness of forest and mountain, lake and river, must ever appear but a weary desolation.

—Warburton Pike, *The Barren Ground of Northern Canada*, 1892

Our progress is sluggish. It is so cold and damp that when we stop for lunch we spread out a huge tarp with everyone underneath, sitting on the edges. The upper portion of the tarp rests on our heads, with the ends tucked in. We pass crackers, dried fruit, and peanuts in the dry and relatively warm confines of the tarp. I am fortunate to be on one end, although it still feels crowded and stuffy. As soon as I finish lunch, I take a walk on the island in the rain. From a distance, the makeshift cafeteria, still full of people, is a sight to behold.

The wind is stiff as the others finally emerge from the tarp. Al is not feeling well and reports some of the symptoms of hypothermia. He is shivering, feeling fatigued, and acting clumsy. We decide to call it a day and paddle just a few hundred yards to a camp spot in a swampy area.

Rain begins to fall again as Dan and I set up the tent. Dan digs deep into his pack. He finds two books for us, for which I am quite grateful, because we will have some time as we wait out the wind. One is titled *What Am I Doing Here?* That title sums up how many in the group are feeling right now.

It is still early afternoon, and we are alerted that if the wind calms down, we will press on and paddle at night. With that in mind, I rest, reading and sleeping, for several hours. The wind continues to howl. After dinner, we are again advised that as soon as the wind abates, we will move on, regardless of the hour. I walk the length of the island and watch Dan haul in a twelve-pound northern pike. We return to camp where everyone is asleep.

~

We are awakened at 5:00 a.m. The wind has finally died down. We break camp in a frenzy and leave without eating breakfast. The water is calm now, but the sky remains dreary. We paddle for a few hours with little conversation. Then we pull the canoes alongside each other as we rest on the water.

"Pretty country," Leo says to Al, breaking the silence.

"Pretty desolate," Al replies.

How you perceive the landscape depends considerably upon your disposition. This is especially evident in the journals of early explorers. Warburton Pike, in his travels here more than one hundred years ago, described the land as bleak: "the most complete desolation that exists on the face of the earth." Yet in another mood, he described the barrenlands as a "northern fairyland" and declared: "A man who has spent much time under the influence of the charm which the north exercises over everybody wants nothing better than to be allowed to finish his life in the peace and quietness which reign by the shores of the Great Slave Lake." For now, Al is hungry and tired, like the rest of us. His sense of wonder will return.

Eventually, the inevitable question is raised: "When are we going to eat?" Everyone is famished, and we spot relatively level terrain a few minutes paddle in the direction from which we came. But Leo (and I happen to share this trait) does not like to go backward. His preference is made clear: "I hate to lose ground."

We land at a steeper site consistent with the direction we're traveling. Someone picks up the lunch pack, takes a few steps up the near-vertical embankment, and falls down. We are too hungry to take the time to cook up hot cereal. Instead we wolf down our standard lunch fare for breakfast.

After our meal, we continue paddling upriver. We stop in a narrow length of the channel just below Cook Lake. It is too gusty to continue, so we wait for a break in the wind. To pass the time, someone casts a line into the current and immediately hauls in a large lake trout. This encourages several others to grab their fishing gear, as the sun begins breaking through the clouds. With four or five people fishing, at any given time, two or three may be reeling in trout.

Having already consumed our lunch, we cook up trout and potatoes for an afternoon dinner. We are windbound, and that means some time to slow down, some time for ourselves—the upside of adversity. The wind also means fewer airborne mosquitoes. With this leisure, I bathe, launder clothes, hike, take photographs, and nap in the sun.

By evening we are once again hungry, so we eat our missing meal—a breakfast of granola and Grapenuts. The wind finally subsides, and we paddle into the evening and the rich light at the end of the day. It is breezy, but not too strong, and the temperature is ideal for paddling.

I couldn't feel much better after a long afternoon of rest. But my friend and colleague, Dan Dustin—the only other person beside Leo I knew prior to this trip—couldn't feel worse. Dustin notifies Leo that he is not feeling well, and that he will ease up on paddling. After another mile or so, we pull to shore for him.

Dustin walks a short distance then settles down on the tundra among clouds of mosquitoes. Although the evening is warm, he is shaking uncontrollably. I go to his duffle to get his sleeping bag, then set up his tent with Leo. We hustle him into the tent before too many mosquitoes and black flies can join him.

Dustin feels a sharp pain in his side. His symptoms include nausea, vomiting, and diarrhea. In a tiny copse of spruce, we set up a tarp that blocks the view, near his tent, so he has a semblance of privacy in coping with his misery.

Each of us hold theories as to what may be causing Dustin such distress. Could it be food poisoning? A severe allergic reaction to all the insect bites? Is it appendicitis or some rare condition that without prompt medical attention could be life threatening? We don't know.

7

No Rescue Wilderness

Leo and Dustin were graduate students together at the University of Minnesota. Leo, after completing his doctorate, accepted a faculty position there. Dustin took a position at San Diego State University. But they stayed in touch.

In academia, you publish or perish, and these two collaborated to publish much of their work. They share a professional interest in wilderness management, conservation education, and environmental ethics. Inspired by the thinking of Robert Marshall, they have a particular passion for promoting recreationist self-sufficiency in wilderness. And among other things, they have advocated establishing a no rescue wilderness area. A no rescue wilderness is just what it sounds like—a place where the federal land management agency would not establish and offer rescue services.

These scholars believe the wilderness experience available in many of our national parks and national forests has been tainted. Many of the most popular wilderness areas, at least in the continental United States, suffer from crowding. As more and more people converge on a wilderness area, various management strategies must be adopted. For example, a limit on use is often established. This means only those people who have applied for and secured permits may venture into the area. Wilderness managers have also found it necessary to enforce many rules and regulations. The rules help protect the landscape and are essential, but they come at the expense of traditional outdoor recreation liberties. In some wilderness areas, certain places are off limits. In others, wilderness users are assigned where they camp. All of this takes away from the freedom, the challenge, and the adventure of a wilderness experience.

Leo and Dustin proposed a no rescue wilderness in a portion of Gates of the Arctic National Park and Preserve. This enormous national park is in the Brooks Range of northern Alaska, where Robert Marshall explored the landscape more than a half-century ago. Marshall earned his PhD in plant pathology at Johns Hopkins University. He studied the adaptations of tundra plants to the harsh landscape of the Brooks Range. He noted that only plants well adapted to the severe conditions could survive.

This location has been purposely chosen. Gates of the Arctic is very remote and mostly unvisited. Only well-seasoned wilderness travelers have the outdoor knowledge and skills to venture there. The idea is to keep this area relatively uncrowded and unregulated. People who wanted to spend time there would have to be completely self-sufficient. Just as tundra plants are adapted to the extreme conditions, wilderness users would need expert knowledge and skills to face the rigors of the environment.

In *Coming into the Country*, published in 1976, author John McPhee recounts the perspective of a National Park Service planner involved for years with study and planning for Gates of the Arctic: "[His] total plans for the park's development—his intended use of airstrips, roadways, lodges, leantos, refreshment stands, trash barrels, benches—added up to zero. The most inventive thing to do, as he saw it, was nothing. Let the land stand wild, without so much as a man-made trail."

Only the federal government would be restricted from search and rescue efforts, which, simply, would not be established. Obviously, members of a group would do what was possible to save a comrade. The emphasis of the policy is directed at preventing the government from getting involved.

Search and rescue efforts cost the National Park Service millions of dollars per year. This expense is of concern to some people. The National Taxpayers Union, a Washington-based group that advocates less government spending, notes that individuals who intentionally put themselves in danger should foot the bill. Their position is that taxpayers should not subsidize thrill seekers. The existence of rescue services may encourage adventurers to take on more than they are capable of.

The National Park Service has considered requiring mountain climbers, whitewater river runners, and others engaged in high-risk recreation to pay for their own rescues but dropped the idea. What if someone couldn't afford the rescue? Subsequently, some select parks, including Denali National Park and Preserve in Alaska, have instituted registration fees. This money is pooled (like insurance) and used to help finance rescues.

However, the crux of the issue transcends saving money. The idea is philosophical. The proposed no rescue wilderness is a statement. It is a stand in favor of those who want to take full responsibility for their actions. Leo and Dustin believe the proposal is an affirmation of the sanctity of life—what it means to live.

Although philosophically consistent with wilderness ideals, the no rescue wilderness proposal has not been well received. Some opponents have pointed out that such an uncontrolled area would be an invitation for people to take their lives. I suspect if troubled individuals went to the bother of going all the way to Gates of the Arctic to die by suicide, they would be so inspired by the country—the mountains, the rivers, the wildlife—they would want to live after all. These individuals may well return home with a passion for the goodness of life.

Other arguments against the proposal suggest the federal government would be liable for those who were badly injured or killed. Legal scholars have looked at the issue and have suggested that if potential users are made aware of the no rescue status of the area through park information services, then it would be highly unlikely that the National Park Service would be held liable for injuries or deaths in such a place.

Leo and Dustin are quick to point out that most people are drawn immediately to what might go wrong rather than focusing on what may go right for those who would *choose* to enter such an area. Experienced wilderness users would thrive, almost exclusively, given arrangements where they assumed their own responsibility.

Should wilderness enthusiasts today be allowed the choice of total self-sufficiency in this one place? In deciding for or against this proposal, there is a bottom line that is inescapable. You couldn't change your mind.

The most vehement opponents to a no rescue wilderness insist that those foolish enough to choose such adventure would surely regret the decision if they got in trouble. The picture that is painted is one of desperation; pathetic depictions of people regretful, panicked, and afraid to die. I believe this perspective shines light on the fears of those who oppose the idea and not those who might choose such an experience.

There are those who are willing to go out into the world, to take risks, and to grow in the process. There are those who will risk losing their lives in order to gain them. At a memorial service I attended not long ago, the minister said we should not be afraid to die, we should not be afraid of dying, and we should not be afraid to live. The more fully we embrace life, the easier it is to die, because we have lived.

But what if Dustin—of all people—who came up with the idea and is terribly ill out here in the wilderness, really were on the doorstep of death? Would he grovel madly about his regrets? Or would his message be something else?

I know Dustin well, and I believe he would die with integrity. I have taken the liberty to estimate what he might do and say. First, he would say farewell to and clear away the others, asking that just Leo and I remain, the two who have known him the longest. Dustin would have special words for us to convey to his beloved, Kathy. I won't attempt to second-guess those words. He would mention many friends. But the focus of his words would be on his boys. Dustin might say:

Tell Andy and Adam that I love them. They know. Tell them that I am proud of them; they are wonderful sons, and they mean the world to me. Tell them that if not for pushing myself, I wouldn't be the father I am, I would be something much less than that. I want them to affirm life and know what it means to live. So, ask the boys to cherish their lives, but not be afraid to live their lives. Tell them to take chances. To risk failure. It is the only way to grow. Tell them to celebrate my life and to recall those special times we have spent together. I will live on in the memory of those shared experiences. I will also live on in the words of my books and those who have been influenced by those words. And in the lives of my students. And my friends.

Dustin would say to reassure his boys that the show must go on. He would ask Leo and I to look out for them as best we could.

Knowing Dustin as I do, it is conceivable that he would say something funny. He might quote Robert Service or John Muir or Henry David Thoreau. He would offer keen insight. He would teach not only what it means to live but what it means to die.

No, the scene would not be pathetic but rather one of wisdom and courage. We are all going to die and there are worse ways to go—say, in a hospital hooked up to all sorts of technology among strangers—than in the beauty of the wilderness among friends. Dustin would express gratitude for the life he lived. Then he would show anticipation for the next adventure, one bigger than all the rest.

Dustin wrote in *The Wilderness Within*, "To me, wilderness is the logical place, indeed the ideal place, to marvel at life's unfolding, to live at life's edge. It is in wilderness that we can best discard the protective armor that shields us from life itself. It is in wilderness that we can best rejoice in the here and now."

~

The next morning we get a late start out of consideration for Dustin's condition. Still in pain after a miserable night, he rides motionless in the bow of a canoe. Cook Lake is perfectly still, providing a mirror image of the cloud formations above.

We arrive at our first portage around the rapids of the Hoarfrost River. What appears to be a short portage is three-quarters of a mile. Due to the calmness of the day, the mosquitoes and blackflies are horrendous. I shoulder a canoe with Leo past sparkling, cascading waters.

As several of us return to pick up another load, Al breaks into song as we cross a mosquito-infested swamp. With shoulders hunched, knees lifting high, hips swiveling, and fingers snapping he sings about the dreaded insects:

"Mosquitoes in the morning, mosquitoes in the evening, mosquitoes at supper time . . ."

The next portage around rapids is perhaps one hundred yards. Aki has caught up with us and he "lines" his sea kayak; pulling it behind him, with a rope. Leo is tempted to line the canoes—to avoid having to completely unload, carry just a short distance, and reload—but Al is against it.

Leo and I decide to line our canoe in the water anyway. With Leo pulling from the bow and with me pushing from the stern, we maneuver the canoe upstream against a swift current. My boots feel as if they are filled with cement as we clamber over slippery boulders, up to the waist in icy water. It is a wonder we aren't swept away.

The group continues paddling upstream. The next obstacle is a chute of fast water. The canoe ahead of us crosses the torrent near the top of the rapid. We follow their lead without contemplating the hazards. We paddle the canoe properly, at a slight angle and maintaining momentum, to avoid turning over in the swift water. Still, I can feel the craft almost flip as we hit the forceful current. For the canoe to swamp at this moment would be a disaster. It is inconceivable that we wouldn't have lost some of our cargo downriver. Furthermore, a dunking is the last thing Dustin needs. We are lucky.

Further along, and after a tiresome portage, we make camp out of consideration for Dustin, who continues to suffer. Most everyone is exhausted, sitting around next to their packs, in a stupor. Before long, Dan and I look around for a tent site. As we pitch the tent he says, "I'd sure like a drink of water."

I REPLY, WITH UNREASONABLE HOPE, "I'D SURE LIKE A BEER."

Within moments, Olesen's plane comes into view. He circles twice, then lands on the water. He has brought his wife, Kristen, to meet us. He has also brought us fourteen cans of beer. We cook up a feast of falafel (a Middle Eastern food), breaded and soy trout, rice, and pudding. The atmosphere is like a party. The blackflies and mosquitoes are dreadful, but go unacknowledged, without a complaint from anyone.

I talk with Kristen, who works as a cook at a drilling site on George Lake (named after explorer George Back). Like her husband, Kristen is tall and lean.

Aki breaks out a map and shows several of us the trips he has completed throughout the Northwest Territories. He calls the north "a treasure" and assures us that he will be back next summer for his annual meditation.

Amid all the festivity, Dustin recuperates in his tent. Leo and Olesen consider Dustin's symptoms and decide to let him stay rather than flying him out from here. (As it turns out, Dustin was likely suffering from a condition known as diverticulitis, a painful but common malady. After experiencing similar symptoms, he was diagnosed with this illness after our return.)

Before long, Olesen and his wife are ready to go home. They haven't seen each other for a month, which is not uncommon during the summer. Their little time together is precious. Kristen will be back tomorrow to accompany us for the remainder of the journey. The plane takes off from the water and they fly low past our camp. I watch until the plane is out of sight, then eat the last of my trout and finish my beer.

Content, I settle down to sleep, listening to the gentle cascades of the Hoarfrost River.

8

The Country, the Space, the Sky

He makes me lie down in green pastures, He leads me beside still waters,

He restores my soul.

—Psalm 23:2-3

The following morning, we paddle a short distance, then complete a half-mile portage. I have pulled a muscle in my back and find it excruciating to lift even the lightest load. Once something is on my back, however, I can transport it without too much agony. After some success hauling packs, I think I might be able to carry a canoe. One is gently eased onto my shoulders, and I feel a sharp pain, like a knife in my back. I wince as the full weight rests on my shoulders. Al says that all he had to do was look at my face to realize that carrying a canoe over this and the last portage would be out of the question. What is far worse than the heavy work, I think, is not being able to do the heavy work.

We paddle a short distance upstream to face the last portage, of eighteen total, on the trip. Olesen and Kristen arrive and land their plane on the calm water of Walmsley Lake.

This portage around rapids is a short one, and the canoes are quickly moved and then reloaded. The sun is shining, and a light breeze blows as we gather for a group photo. Then Olesen has something to say to us.

He speaks slowly and deliberately. We are gathered in a quarter moon around him, with Kristen further away by the water. Olesen recounts the highlights of our voyage from Yellowknife to Walmsley Lake, more than 270 miles. The people who will come to use these canoes, he says, will appreciate our efforts, although only we know, really, the hardships of the journey.

He acknowledges the difficulty of our task, the inclement weather, the notion that no one else, save Aki, has ever traversed this route. The canoes will not be returned to Great Slave Lake, he explains, but will be stored along a lakeshore somewhere in the barrenlands. Our group is uncharacteristically silent, focused on his words, which are heartfelt.

He says, "A bunch of young yahoos probably couldn't have done what you did. It took your maturity, your experience, and your perseverance to see the expedition through." He knows we have pushed throughout the entire trip and that several of us are sick or injured.

Olesen goes on to apologize for not getting to know us better, there not being ample opportunity to become friends, although he is open to that in the future. He invites us to come back to use the canoes, to put together a trip. He assures us, "As you look back upon this trip, you will miss the country, the space, the sky." We are welcome, he repeats, to return.

His love for this land and his admiration for what we have done are evident. Choked with emotion now, he adds, "Thanks a lot for all you have done." His breath catches in his throat. He looks down. Kristen, from a distance, is smiling gently at him. As he turns and walks away, Leo thanks him for all he has done for us. Olesen just keeps walking. As he passes Kristen, he pauses for just a moment, then walks to his plane. She follows him. After exchanging a private farewell, he paddles his plane to deeper water, to prepare for takeoff. We will not see him again.

We launch the canoes and ferry up the narrow channel in single file as Olesen motors up the lake ahead of us. Kristen has joined our canoe and is seated in front of me, beyond the gear.

After lifting off the water, Olesen circles us, then flies directly overhead in the direction of his cabin. In unison, we raise our paddles to the sky in tribute to a strong and gentle man—a fifteen-paddle salute.

We are now on Walmsley Lake, and there is a wind behind us for the first time. We stop for lunch on an island. The breeze is sufficient to curb the mosquitoes. According to the map, we have made it beyond the northern boundary where trees grow. I hurry through lunch, then walk to the end of the island where I sit alone. Aside from the breeze and water lapping the shore, there is no sound, although Olesen's words still ring in my ears. Yes, I am sure I will miss all of this: the country, the space, the sky.

The country: I am in a verdant pasture of tundra greenery, reclining among lichens of all shades and a bed of tiny pink flowers. This land supports wolves and caribou, grizzlies and moose. Further north, still, there are polar bears and prehistoric-looking muskoxen.

The space: In the distance I see other islands in this huge expanse of water. I can see so far that it appears the lake drops off the end of the world. There isn't a tree in sight. The landscape seems to reach to eternity.

The sky: Overhead, the sun is partially obscured by a cumulus cloud. I count twenty beams of light radiating, like divine fingers of light, out of the heavens. Glory be to God.

Indeed, the moment turns magic in the harmony of the country, the space, the sky. A tear wells slowly in one eye, then the other.

After lunch we paddle toward our destination, Maufelly Bay. We spot two moose, a cow and her calf, swimming in front of the canoes. As they reach shore, they burst out of the water, bucking and kicking up spray, then run up and over a ridge, the calf fast on the hooves of its mother.

Aki drifts farther and farther back until he is out of sight. There will be no farewell, for we will not see him again. His departure is as subtle and undramatic as his appearance was sudden.

We land on a point at the mouth of Maufelly Bay about five miles short of our destination. After dinner, several of us pick cranberries in a bog. The sky is ever changing, shifting from aquamarine to an unusual purple hue.

9

Wolf Pups

In the morning, we eat tart cranberry pancakes. We launch the canoes for the last leg of our journey under gray skies. As we paddle, Leo confides in me that he is tired, both physically and emotionally. Over the course of the expedition, we have talked about our lives, our loved ones, what the future holds, various aspects of the trip—but mostly we are silent, something we are both comfortable with. However, a routine developed, not purposely, whereby several times each day one or the other of us would remark about the beauty of the land, the other person always nodding in agreement.

As we come upon a grim-looking island, Leo says, "That looks like Alcatraz."

I have never heard of Alcatraz Island referred to in sublime terms. Indeed Leo, like the rest of us, is tired.

Before long, we see our goal, the place we agreed to leave the canoes. The two other craft, ahead of us, land on an island, thinking it is the mainland. One of the canoeists throws his life jacket on the ground and kicks it, apparently relieved that the ordeal is over. We motion the other canoes on as we pass them and land at our last camp.

With all three canoes now on shore, there are handshakes, hoots, and tears. Leo and Al embrace. After a short while, amid considerable excitement, I am summoned to the top of a ridge. Hiking over the promontory, I see a wolf den about a quarter mile away. We keep our distance, high on the ridge, as we look down upon five young pups, a few months old. Members of our group come and go as they find out about the wolves. The pups shift around occasionally, but mostly sleep in piles of two or three. Now and then, one will get up, stretch, and move to another pile.

Leo and I watch, both amazed and thankful for the solitude, that everyone in our party is not up on the ridge. One pup enters the den, only to reemerge later. At the entrance of the den, the pup turns its nose to the sky and howls—a long, mournful wail toward the full moon on the horizon. The pile of wolf pups increases from two, to three, to four. Then the last one joins the pack, crawling over, and settling on top of the others. Finally, one by one, they go into the den for the night. Once all the pups are in the den, we return to camp for dinner.

I eat quickly, wash a few pots and pans, fill my canteen, and return to the ridge. I am astonished, indeed overwhelmed, with what we have stumbled upon. I am hoping for a glimpse of an adult. Later in the night, Leo joins me. We sit and watch a long while before retiring.

~

This last full day, I take a hike with Dustin, who has now mostly recovered from his illness. We meet up with Leo a good distance from camp.

In the evening, we are hit by a ferocious squall. The blast is cold, the rain is steady. Dan's tent can take no more, the middle pole snaps, and it collapses completely. We haul the tent, with a filling of sleeping bags and personal gear, under the awning of our closest neighbors and wait out the storm, telling stories in their tent. After the storm, we fix Dan's tent so it will survive the last night, eat fish chowder for dinner, then fall asleep.

Arrangements have been made for flying back to Yellowknife, and we will be picked up by a Twin Otter later in the day. After breakfast, I watch the wolf pups explore the terrain that lies within a few hundred yards of the den. They explore independently, then reconvene to nap in piles. Now and again, they cry out. Later, I make a loop hike, alone. I stop often, full of wonder. Sometimes I walk a couple hundred yards before pausing. Other times I move forward only a few steps before stopping to look around again. The scene changes constantly: The country. The space. The sky. I am wearing a flannel shirt, sweater, vest, and parka—in July. It is a blustery day with occasional sprinkles.

Once again, along a quiet water's edge, I listen closely to the breath of the wind and nothing else.

10

The Way of Adventure

A wilderness experience is about time and space. Initially, we must allocate time to break away. This can be the greatest challenge—setting aside time for something we know will bring a special dimension to our lives. We must instruct and discipline ourselves to make room for adventure that may enrich us beyond our dreams.

The adventure itself is like an extended Sabbath—a sabbatical. A sabbatical is both a time of rest and a time of ambitious creative pursuit. Similarly, adventure in our lives allows us to leave behind routine chores to actively pursue a different agenda. Part of what is so rejuvenating is the contrast to day-to-day activities and the luxury of intense focus.

A wilderness experience is also dependent upon unexploited, unmanaged, and seemingly unlimited space. We find harmony of form and color and life as we fall into resonance with ancient rhythms. On this trip, we were inspired by the stark beauty of a land beyond treeline.

In wilderness, we may wonder about the adaptations of various organisms to their environment and the relationships that exist among species. One of the highlights of this journey was watching the wolf pups at play. I observed an innocence, unimaginable in our everyday lives, that is completely oblivious to our existence, and yet, in many ways, is dependent upon the integrity of our actions.

On this trip, we were exposed firsthand to a land almost untouched. This was a history lesson without parallel. The past came to life as we practiced tasks from centuries ago. We cooked over open fires, paddled the lakes and rivers, and heard the same haunting calls of the loons. We knew the same vast horizons and the ever-changing patterns of the sky.

The very nature of a wilderness adventure suggests challenge and risk. Such experiences are exhilarating, and we have a greater sense of being alive. We push ourselves in wilderness to reach a goal: the top of a mountain, the depths of a canyon, a far lake. We strive hard to do something with the faith that it is worth the effort.

Yet a price is paid, and that is part of the point. Across the board our group faced various ailments on this trip, and everyone was physically exhausted and emotionally drained by the end. Had it been a relaxing fishing excursion, it wouldn't have been the same; it wouldn't have meant as much.

Hardship is part of the experience, indeed part of the attraction. An adventure without difficulty is a contradiction. A life without trial is not fully lived. The storms of our lives lend themselves to fear, anger, self-pity, and despair or an expanded degree of gratitude for what we do have, which translates into a sense of peace, serenity, thanksgiving, and joy.

Wilderness adventure can elicit deep emotional responses. It can generate a sense of clarity and truth. Such adventure may overwhelm the senses, prompt consideration of new priorities, assist in confronting adversity, initiate a generous response, or inspire a courageous course of action. Exposure to a wild landscape may encourage a less complex, less stressful, less consumptive way of life. A wilderness odyssey can generate a sense of hope, of seeing the good in life through all the bad.

We need the contrast of adventure in our lives—some adventure—to complement our day-to-day routines and obligations. Both are essential for our well-being, as are solitude and community, focused effort and relaxation, affliction and triumph. In wilderness, we can *move beyond* what we are accustomed to seeing, feeling, thinking, and doing into new territory of the landscape and the mind.

More than a vacation—a respite, a travelogue—we return home to see things differently. We are inspired now, as agents of change, to move beyond the old way of doing things to seeing a new way, bringing a life-affirming perspective to a world in need.

Amid the quiet and power of wilderness, we may test and rest our minds and bodies and find our souls restored.

Have you gazed on naked grandeur where there's nothing else to gaze on,
Set pieces and drop-curtain scenes galore,
Big mountains heaved to heaven, which the blinding sunsets blazon,
Black canyons where the rapids rip and roar?
Have you swept the visioned valley with the green stream streaking through it,
Searched the Vastness for a something you have lost?
Have you strung your soul to silence? Then for God's sake go and do it;
Hear the challenge, learn the lesson, pay the cost.

—Robert Service

Part II
And Other Stories

Barry Lopez

LEADING BY STORY

Barry Lopez died on Christmas Day, 2020. Three weeks later I saw the news at the bottom of a *Los Angeles Times* newsfeed called "The Wild." Engulfed in a cascade of thoughts and emotions, I was perplexed that this great man's passing had not received more recognition and that it took so long for me to find out.

Lopez is one of the foremost leaders, through his storytelling over four decades, of how we think about culture, especially Indigenous culture, and, related to that, how we behave toward the natural world. Lopez won numerous literary honors including the National Book Award for Nonfiction.

In *The Gifts of Interpretation*, Ted Cable and I refer to Lopez nine times, more than anyone else except for Enos Mills and Freeman Tilden. Lopez wrote in 2016, "We regularly forget what we want our lives to mean. . . . We repeatedly lose touch with what we intend our lives to stand for. To protect us, the elders must constantly reacquaint us with our ideals." Upon reflection, this is ultimately the role of those who interpret nature, history, and culture—they are the elders who reacquaint people with their ideals.

ON STORY

As I tried to find solace I selected a book, *Crow and Weasel*, published in 1993, from the top of a bookshelf where I have much of everything Lopez wrote, an extraordinary body of work, fiction and nonfiction. I opened the book randomly to this passage where a character, Badger, says, "The stories people tell have a way of taking care of them. If stories come to you, care for them. And learn to give them away where they are needed. Sometimes a person needs a story more than food to stay alive." Interpreters, clearly, have a great deal to offer in taking care of, and giving away, stories. This, then, is the gift of story—interpreters leading people to not stray from what they intend their lives to stand for.

As I pulled other books off the shelf, I remembered an essay in *Crossing Open Ground*, published in 1989, titled "Grown Men," and turned to it. Here Lopez pays tribute to three men who were mentors to him at various times in his life, who had all died recently. His words reverberated with emotions I was feeling at the very moment. He wrote early in the essay, "It had been a year for deaths."

Yes, I pondered, a year for deaths. In 2020, we were shellshocked by death. Hundreds of thousands nationwide and two million worldwide died in the throes of a pandemic, made worse by national leadership that didn't pay attention to the medical science. Icons of civil rights and social justice, Ruth Bader Ginsburg and John Lewis, authentic leaders, were lost to cancer. More personal, my closest friend's twenty-four-year-old son died by suicide as this brutal year came toward a close. And then, on Christmas Day, Lopez passed away from cancer.

I felt that same agony of loss that Lopez described in "Grown Men," over the deaths of the past year, "as though the piers had suddenly gone out from under the veranda of an ancestral southern home and revealed it abandoned."

The men that Lopez wrote about represented qualities he thought were vanishing. He wrote, "I realized just before they died that there was something of transcendent value in them, fragile and as difficult to extract as the color of a peach."

But the character of these men did emerge in his accounting of them as kindness, clear-headedness, responsibility, humility, generosity, integrity, persistence in the face of trouble, a gentle sense of humor—all qualities, as I brooded over his death, that to me characterized Lopez himself, all elements of effective leadership.

ON SPENDING TIME WITH LOPEZ

My introduction to Lopez was at a book signing in Minneapolis, in 1986, where I was attending graduate school. I found *Arctic Dreams: Imagination and Desire in a Northern Landscape* displayed in the local bookstore with notice of Lopez's upcoming event. Even the brief encounter as he signed my book evidenced his intensity and grace. I had recently spent time working in Alaska and quickly immersed myself in the eloquence and sublimity of Lopez's words.

Three years later I invited Lopez, on behalf of my university, to be part of a lecture series called "Promoting Environmental Messages through the Arts." As his host, I had the luxury of spending three days with Lopez. When I picked him up at precisely the time we had arranged, the first morning, he was waiting outside his motel. He said to me, "You're thirty seconds late." When I turned to him sharply, he was smiling impishly. He was toying with me.

I wrote an essay about our time together titled "Conversations with Barry Lopez: Musings on Interpretation," which was published in the *Journal of Interpretation* (the precursor to *Legacy*) in 1989. I sent the article to Lopez, and he sent a kind card in reply. We exchanged a few telephone calls and letters, but because of my negligence the budding friendship didn't get off the ground.

Of the seemingly countless nuggets of wisdom that I wrote down from my conversations with Lopez, one was this: "It is a terrific struggle to be a decent human being." One of the other things I learned from Lopez, reading his work over the following years, was that his most powerful essays, at least for me, were those when he revealed something of himself.

ON LIFE'S CHALLENGES

Lopez wrote his most personal and harrowing story in the January 2013 issue of *Harper's Magazine*. This is the soul-wrenching account of when he was sexually abused, by a friend of his mother, as a young boy over the course of several years, starting at the age of seven. Lopez was petrified to say anything about his rapist who purported to be a doctor, which later proved to be fraudulent. At the hands of a serial pedophile, who claimed medical authority that was respected by fellow adults, Lopez felt helpless and sought refuge in the natural world.

Terry Gross, of National Public Radio's *Fresh Air* series, interviewed Lopez in 2013 on why he finally told a story he had withheld through most of his adult life and how the outside world helped him cope with the turmoil of his inner one. Lopez said, "I know this: That when I was so compromised as a child that there was no zone of safety for me. . . . I saw something outside myself, the world beyond the self . . . and I felt this surge of lyrical pleasure in the way the wind sounded, for example, in eucalyptus trees."

Now, returning to the essay "Grown Men," Lopez wrote about the three men he admired and longed for: "For men who had had difficult times . . . they were uncommonly free of bitterness. There was a desire in them to act to help when something went wrong rather than to assign blame, even when the trouble was over. When something went very wrong, they reached down into a reservoir of implacable conviction, as a man puts his hands into a cold, clear basin of water."

Lopez continued, "I wanted to speak with them. Because there are lives, near and distant, wearing out too quickly, without plan or laughter."

ON LOVE

Lopez wrote the foreword to a book published by the Orion Society, in 2020, titled *Earthly Love: Stories of Intimacy and Devotion*. His is the lead piece in a book of essays by other luminary writers and poets appropriate, I think, because his work stands apart, and, importantly, some of his peers have acknowledged this.

Lopez wouldn't approve of me saying so, but, again, others have agreed, he is in a class of his own. In his foreword, Lopez explained how he "experienced what it meant to love" over the course of summer days with friends in the Brooks Range of Alaska observing wolves and caribou and bears, not "wild" animals he would instruct but rather "free." The experience "delivered" him to the central project of his adult life as a writer, "which is to know and love what we have been given, and to urge others to do the same."

His essay concludes, "In this trembling moment . . . with fires roaring across the vineyards of California . . . with Niagaras of water falling into the oceans from every sector of Greenland, in this moment, is it still possible to face the gathering darkness, and say to the physical Earth, and to all its creatures, including ourselves, fiercely and without embarrassment, I love you, and to embrace fearlessly the burning world?"

AFTERWORD

After reading *Horizon*, his most recent book, a five-hundred-page masterpiece published in 2019, my intent was to write and tell Lopez what our brief time together, and all his writings, have meant to me. But I hesitated too long, got caught up in other things, things that don't seem so important now. Or to be both more honest and more precise, I was remiss. I feel the weight of that failure, like bricks, that exacerbates my sadness. But I know I must heed this mentor, "embrace fearlessly the burning world," then look, with ever more clarity and sense of purpose, to the horizon.

AUTHOR'S NOTE

Several of my friends and colleagues reviewed this essay for me. There was consensus that interpreters not familiar with Lopez's work might be inspired to seek out his writings. My hope is that this tribute results in more interpreters being exposed to Lopez's wisdom. I recommend two short books to start with: *Crow and Weasel* (fiction) and *The Rediscovery of North America* (nonfiction). Longer works that I found particularly meaningful include *About This Life* and *Horizon* (both nonfiction).

Running for Our Lives

Brian Doyle (2019) wrote, in an essay titled "On Not 'Beating' Cancer," that "cancer is a dance partner you don't want and don't like, but you have to dance, and either you die or the cancer fades back into the darkness at the other end of the ballroom."

I know that dance partner. Only a few days into the new millennium, in January 2000, I was diagnosed with cancer, a form of lymphoma that doesn't have a cure. As with many cancer patients, I went through surgery. There were CT scans, PET scans, MRIs, bone marrow biopsies, and radiation treatments. I didn't want or like this dance partner, but I understood "you have to dance, and either you die or the cancer fades back . . ."

When I was able, I'd run in the morning before work at my sons' elementary school in a program called "Run for Fun." The kids and many parents ran around a track before school started. I cherished those runs, outdoors in the crisp air, engulfed in the rhapsody of children's laughter; they were the highlight of my day.

For several years I was in remission, then my ominous dance partner came back. I went through the legion of hoops to enter a clinical trial that might cure my cancer. Then, at the last moment, I was pulled out of the trial and entered an unnerving period known as "watch and wait" when there is nothing to be done for a particular cancer pending further symptoms.

Approximately every ten minutes someone dies from lymph or blood cancers, the second leading cause of cancer deaths in the United States. The Leukemia and Lymphoma Society (LLS) raises funds to research cures for these systemic cancers through several different long-distance athletic events. In cooperation with Team in Training, participants raise funds for cancer research while training for half marathons, full marathons, one-hundred-mile bike rides, and triathlons.

As I gained strength, I set my sights on completing a marathon while at the same time raising funds for LLS to find cures. My oncologist gave the okay.

Running can be good medicine.

ARIZONA ROCK 'N' ROLL MARATHON

I enrolled to raise funds and train for the Arizona Rock 'N' Roll Marathon. We had a training program that included "team" runs on Saturday mornings, where we gradually gained mileage on various local courses, and a program for individual work during the rest of the week.

On the "team" runs I asked others why they were doing this, which was often to honor someone battling the disease or in memory of someone who died. Some stories I heard were devastating.

Alyce was about my same speed, so we talked a lot. She told me about losing her son Samuel. She explained how Samuel seemed like a perfectly healthy baby. But later he cried incessantly and insisted on being held, even when he slept, which baffled her. She was concerned and took Samuel to the hospital, but it seems his condition was misdiagnosed, and he was sent home. So Alyce would cuddle Samuel not knowing at the time about the disease that would take his life, the pain he was in that he couldn't express, and the comfort he took from his mother's warmth.

As the complications persisted Alyce took Samuel back to the hospital. It was a Wednesday and the baby, this time, was diagnosed with leukemia. Chemotherapy was started that same day. But Samuel died on Sunday. He was eight weeks old.

Alyce told me about Samuel's four-year-old brother who, rattled in the aftermath, couldn't comprehend what happened. For some time after he searched the house, everywhere, looking for his baby brother.

Each Saturday, prior to setting out on our course for the day, someone provided a Mission Moment. This was always a heartfelt story of someone's connection to the disease, meant to reinforce the importance of our cause. On this day Alyce spoke about Samuel.

As she began, I was concerned she'd never make it through to the end. Sure enough, about halfway, Alyce broke down sobbing. After being consoled by our coaches, she was somehow able to finish, at which point everyone was in tears. She told us she wanted to raise funds for a cure so some other young mother would never have to go through what she had, to see her baby die from this disease, and have her heart broken.

SAN DIEGO ROCK 'N' ROLL MARATHON

After completing my first marathon I was so inspired by the people I met—and their stories of grace under duress—that I was determined to do it again, six months later. This time it would be the San Diego Rock 'N' Roll Marathon.

Here I learned of Kati who battled leukemia throughout her childhood and was eventually approached by the Make-A-Wish Foundation as her condition worsened. As a measure of her character, she turned them down, suggesting they grant another child's wish. But later the Foundation persisted, and Kati said "Yes."

At the time, Kati was the "Honored Teammate" for an LLS chapter of runners in Maryland raising money for cancer cures. Her wish, then, was to come to San Diego's marathon to watch "her" runners cross the finish line. Weighing only fifty pounds at the time because of the disease that was consuming her, she cheered from the finish line, then turned to her father and said, "Dad, I can do this too."

A runner must be sixteen years old to run in one of these marathons. After 109 weeks of chemotherapy, Kati died at the age of fourteen.

But the year Kati would have turned sixteen her father came back to San Diego to run the race for her. Kati's father was one of our keynote speakers the night before the marathon—in a large convention center ballroom—and he spoke of his daughter's inextinguishable courage. He said about her cancer: "She never let it change her. She never let it dim her view. She still loved life, rather than hating the circumstance."

In an unprecedented move, Kati's father was able to get two timing chips from race officials. One recorded his finishing time. The other recorded the same time for Kati. She was listed as having finished the marathon.

CARLSBAD HALF MARATHON

Years later I committed to a half marathon after having lunch with Carol, a former student of mine at San Diego State University. Carol had been the "Outstanding Graduating Senior" in our program the year she graduated, having the highest GPA. I was aware that shortly after graduation, while working for the National Park Service (NPS), Carol was diagnosed with Hodgkin's lymphoma. She went through all sorts of tests and treatments including radiation and chemotherapy. She lost all her hair.

The companion who was always at Carol's side throughout her cancer ordeal was her girlfriend Terry, who also worked at Cabrillo National Monument. Now, Carol explained to me at lunch, Terry had just been diagnosed with stage IV lymphoma.

Terry's daughter, Amanda—remarkably—was one of my current students at that time. Amanda had lost her park ranger father to multiple myeloma, yet another blood cancer. She had always dreamed of working for the NPS like her parents. She had already lost her father. Now she was in jeopardy of losing her mother too.

No words can convey the heartache, the anguish, the pain all these women endured because of cancer in their lives. To do something positive and be supportive, Carol and I decided to put together a team to raise funds for LLS and run the Carlsbad Half Marathon in Terry's honor. We called ourselves Team IPA, which stands for India Pale Ale. Our fundraising meetings were held at local craft alehouses. We would celebrate life in the midst of calamity. Team IPA members finished the half marathon on a rainy winter morning. We raised more than $18,000 for cancer research.

Carol has raised funds for LLS and completed more than twenty long-distance events. Terry's medical treatments have been successful. She retired last year from her NPS career. Amanda followed her parents' path, most recently assigned to Sequoia National Park. Sequoias are symbolic of strength, durability, beauty, grandeur, and survival—the same as these three women.

There is one more thing about my former students I must mention. The year she graduated from SDSU, Amanda had the highest GPA and was awarded "Outstanding Graduating Senior," fourteen years after Carol received that same honor.

AFTERWORD

With some trepidation I still see my oncologist every six months for blood work and physicals. When first diagnosed, I realized my future might be short lived. My unwanted dance partner has lurked ever since in the darkness of the ballroom.

But therein may lie a lesson reinforced by an irrepressible little girl who was still cheering up and down at the finish line, who reminds us to appreciate each precious moment. I leave you with thoughts of Kati—dancing on the lip of a gangplank, ocean surging below, salt spray blasting, gulls screeching on the wing, a technicolor sunset blazing on the horizon—rejoicing in the grace and glory of the precarious now.

Reality Matters

LARRY BECK AND DAN DUSTIN

Turning and turning in the widening gyre
The falcon cannot hear the falconer;
Things fall apart; The centre cannot hold.

—William Butler Yeats, 1919

Let us provide an interpretation. Gyre, an oceanographic term, refers to a swirling vortex of air or ocean currents, or in this case the turbulent forces of life itself—spinning between order and mayhem, truth and falsehood, good and evil—that span the human condition. As the vortex widens, as the falcon circles in more distant arcs from the falconer, it loses its bearing, the familiar world upended. A coherent sense of reality crumbles. Things fall apart. Chaos ensues. The center cannot hold. These lines from a poem by Yeats, written just over a century ago at the time of World War I, amid threats from authoritarianism and a pandemic, could not be more pertinent to our times.

INTRODUCTION

We come to this essay with trepidation. Our reality is not precisely the same as the reader's, nor, for that matter, each other's. This is a daunting topic because we cannot offer an American Indian or a Black American or a woman's worldview. We are limited by our own knowledge and experience. But there must be enough commonality in what all of us perceive to be reality, as an entire people, or things fall apart; the center cannot hold.

Philosophers have struggled with the question—What is reality?—from time immemorial. We acknowledge up front that this is a near-impossible topic, for many reasons, not the least of which is the complexity of human nature. Nonetheless, as the adage goes, we all have to face reality, as varied as that reality might be, and there must be some degree of common ground, or the center cannot hold.

A SHIFT IN REALITY

We believe there have been increasingly widening circles in the vortex of reality in recent years. In the past, people got their news from a limited number of sources that, for the most part, held to strict ethical reporting standards. Americans read newspapers in common and tuned in to just a few channels for the nightly news, including Walter Cronkite, a news anchor for two decades referred to as "the most trusted man in America." In those days, we mostly shared a common view of what was real, what was true, what was actually going on in the world. Science and responsible journalism were our gatekeepers of mostly accurate accountings.

This all shifted with the onslaught of fake news, disinformation, conspiracy theories, and outright falsehoods fueled by "news" channels and social media platforms that make profits by stoking their patrons' rage and spreading lies at the expense of the truth. The problem has been exacerbated by the politics of division designed to pit Americans against each other (with a particular aim at historically disenfranchised communities) by manipulating the truth and playing on emotions in ever-widening arcs of deceit to maintain power and gain wealth. The result, to cite a phrase coined by political scientist David C. Barker, is a "marketplace of realities."

Paul Caputo (2020), in his *Legacy* column "Interpretation in a Fact-Free World," noted, "But if [visitors] all arrive with their own set of unique, customized facts—their own reality—how do we even begin to have a conversation?" He concluded, "Interpreters are faced right now with our profession's biggest challenge—being the arbiters of truth in a world without facts."

THE ELEPHANT AT THE INTERPRETIVE SITE

Melinda McFarland, in her 2020 *Legacy* essay "Another Way to Handle Visitors with Politics on Their Minds," wrote, "We cannot pretend that politics is completely separate from interpretation." She discusses climate change at Acadia National Park and the shrinkage of boundaries at Bears Ears National Monument, two volatile issues confounded by the politics of muzzling science and promoting the fossil fuel industry during the Trump administration.

As we contemplate "interpreting reality" we see the political situation continuing to deteriorate. While president, Donald Trump said, "Stick with us. Don't believe the crap you see from these people, the fake news . . . what you're seeing and what you're reading is not what's happening." He not only perpetrated a direct attack on the function of an independent press in a democracy but called for alignment with whatever reality he chose to present. When people purposefully skew reality to meet their own desires or fantasies—political, economic, or otherwise—we are forced into increasing spirals of turbulence.

We know we are stepping into murky waters here. To what degree should we challenge lies that threaten to tear us apart as a nation? Nonetheless, we would be remiss if we left out attacks on reality. The danger in being manipulated by fraudulent claims, and the question of whether to act or not, could not have more serious consequences.

WHAT IS AT STAKE

The spread of disinformation is serious business. The calculated smear of scientific knowledge about COVID-19 resulted in mass illness and death, and disinformation about climate change may result in the greatest disruption of life on earth. At the same time, we are also witnessing attacks on how our past should be taught in public schools. As George Orwell (1949) reminded us in his book *1984*, "Who controls the past controls the future: who controls the present controls the past." If teaching honest history is curtailed in our public schools, as is currently being advanced in several states, then the weight of responsibility falls even more heavily on the interpretive profession to do what needs to be done.

Interpreters are at the forefront of telling a more complete national story to include difficult histories and accomplishments of traditionally marginalized communities, often in the context of social justice advancements that have led our nation to embrace its highest ideals. National Park Service interpretive sites that have opened to the public within the past several years include the Belmont-Paul Women's Equality National Monument, Stonewall National Monument, and Cesar Chavez National Monument. A museum exhibit recognizing Chinese Americans for their contributions to Yosemite National Park has opened to the public.

Smithsonian Museums now include the National Museum of African American History and Culture. Other sites that tell a more complete history of enslavement include the Richmond Slave Trail, Whitney Plantation, Legacy Museum, and the National Memorial for Peace and Justice.

HOW TO EFFECTIVELY AND COMPASSIONATELY INTERPRET REALITY

For a practical guide to interpreting with historical accuracy and scientific integrity—interpreting reality—we turn to Adam Grant, an organizational psychologist. In *Think Again* (2021), Grant challenges the most common defense for a skewed reality: "I'm entitled to my own opinion." Grant's retort is simply: "Yes, we're entitled to hold opinions inside our own heads. If we choose to express them out loud, though, I think it's our responsibility to ground them in logic and facts."

Grant's thinking can be applied to our interpretive profession. He admonishes us to know what we don't know. That way we won't get into trouble for saying something beyond the bounds of our expertise. This requires constant vigilance to stay abreast of current events, paying attention to historical accuracy, and employing authentic science to guard against spreading inaccurate information.

Grant acknowledges that not everything is black and white, and that there are often shades of gray. Within these shades of gray, we should seek to find common ground. Areas of commonality can be sought in our shared values such as equality or democracy or community or health.

Oftentimes, earnest listening results in arriving at areas of common concern. Coming on too strong has the opposite of the desired effect, while asking good questions and carefully listening can generate positive changes. For example, we can ask how people originally formed a certain opinion, which may have been generated without deep reflection or serious thought. Grant suggests, "To help people reevaluate, prompt them to consider how they'd believe different things if they'd been born at a different time or in a different place." This could be especially valuable for those of us interpreting history in these volatile times.

Grant also suggests asking, "What evidence would change your mind?" And then after earnest listening, we can try to shift their thinking on their own terms. To assist people in refining their own beliefs, Grant suggests learning something new from everyone we meet. Seeking new learning is something we interpreters can take advantage of because we meet so many new people every day. Finally, Grant encourages us to make a focused case based on a select few of the strongest points rather than diluting our argument with an onslaught of reasons.

We know interpreters will not be able to reach people who are beyond the vortex of reason. However, fortified by good intent, focused listening, and commitment to historic accuracy and scientific facts, interpreters can reach most people who simply have not paid enough attention to or thought deeply enough about the issues at hand.

CONCLUSION

Interpreters are at the forefront of guiding people at the very origins of our cultural and natural heritage. Interpreters interact with millions of visitors every day. If the nation's citizenry is under siege from disinformation, interpreters can offer a better grip on reality. By focusing on the truth and offering historically accurate and science-based insights, interpreters can counteract the turbulent and widening arc of disinformation, alternative facts, conspiracy theories, and politically motivated lies to prevent things from falling apart, and making sure the center continues to hold.

This may well end up being the interpretive profession's greatest legacy.

Keeping Our Democracy Intact

When we're dancing with the angels, the question will be asked, in 2019, what did we do to make sure we kept our democracy intact? Did we stand on the sidelines and say nothing?

—Elijah Cummings, 2019

Author's Note: This essay was published just a few months after the death of Elijah Cummings in the March/April 2020 themed issue of *Legacy* magazine on "Interpreting Democracy," as America approached the November 2020 presidential election.

Elijah Cummings, born to sharecroppers who fled South Carolina, grew up in a rowhouse in Baltimore. His elementary school did not have basic facilities such as an auditorium. A school counselor advised that he would never become a lawyer. When he was eleven years old, he and other Black children were attacked by a white mob that pelted them with rocks, one that left a life-long scar on his face. Despite the lack of opportunity and mainstream oppression he defied his counselor's advice and graduated from law school. Twenty years later he was sworn into the US Congress. On that day his astonished father wept.

Elijah Cummings served in the House of Representatives for more than twenty years, and at his memorial he was praised as a clearheaded defender of the truth and as someone who earned respect from both parties. His wife, Maya Cummings, said in a 2019 statement, "He worked until his last breath because he believed our democracy was the highest and best expression of our collective humanity and that our nation's diversity was our promise, not our problem."

~

AN EVOLVING DEMOCRACY

Nikole Hannah-Jones (2019), in *The 1619 Project*, reveals "the contradictions and the ideological struggles of a nation founded on both slavery and freedom." She states, "If we are a truly great nation, the truth cannot destroy us."

In one of the most extraordinary stories ever—the story of American democracy—we find a discrepancy between the founding ideals of the world's greatest nation and reality. The principles of liberty and equality, paradoxically, did not apply to everyone. The institution of chattel slavery most dramatically exemplified the hypocrisy. A full and honest reckoning reveals a shameful betrayal in a nation founded on human freedom, yet the oppressed seemed to have faith in a trajectory that would eventually more closely embrace the founding ideals of the nation.

Thus came the Civil War, and an astonishing expansion of human rights that followed, including the Thirteenth Amendment in 1865 (abolishing slavery), the Fourteenth Amendment in 1868 (promising citizenship to those born in the United States and equal protection under the law), and the Fifteenth Amendment in 1870 (providing the right to vote for all men of any race, color, or previous condition of servitude).

Hannah-Jones notes that in this shift in circumstances, the formerly enslaved engaged with the democratic process. During Reconstruction they organized voters, went to the polls, and won legislative seats. But with such gains in civil rights came extreme backlash and another reign of white suppression. This next phase of our "democracy" was known for discrimination, segregation, voter suppression, and lynchings.

Then came the civil rights movement of the 1950s and 1960s. Hannah-Jones shows that through nonviolent actions the very segment of society that had been historically banished was the one to further propel its nation's democratic principles.

Over centuries of hope, resistance, protest, and faith, Black Americans and their allies initiated a shift toward greater freedom and civil rights. Hannah-Jones suggests that in so doing they laid the foundation for other struggles for justice in this country that better matched the meaning of democracy and the rights of an increasingly diverse society.

Our democracy continues to evolve, but not always in positive directions. What have we done, *lately*, as Elijah Cummings asked, to keep our democracy intact? "Did we stand on the sidelines and say nothing?"

We know from our history that advancing our democracy occurs only when citizens "step off the sidelines."

AN INFORMED PUBLIC IN A DEMOCRACY

Interpreters are stewards of the trusted depositories of our heritage. Our interpretive sites tell the American story through firsthand experiences, and

Americans depend on these places to interpret truthfully, scientifically, and with historic accuracy.

In *The Gifts of Interpretation* (2011), Ted Cable and I wrote, "Democracy requires an informed public, and interpreters are a source of knowledge and inspiration in this regard." Good interpretation inspires audience members to think about something or do something they haven't thought about or done before. This includes the provocation to be good citizens in a democracy— to learn more about our cultural and natural heritage and to act upon that knowledge—which is ultimately an act of patriotism.

Interpretive practice can be approached with irrefutable reason that beckons our audiences to better understand the most important ideals of a democracy, and the most important ideals of the interpretive profession, which are the same thing: recognizing the inherent dignity of all people and the sanctity of our land.

THE PEOPLE

A democracy is defined as a system of government by the whole population— of the people, by the people, and for the people. All the people.

The importance of unity permeates our heritage. Our Constitution begins, "We the people," and we are called to form "a more perfect Union." Much of our currency admonishes *e pluribus unum*—out of many, one. Diversity is our strength.

In the early stages of our democracy George Washington, in his 1796 "Farewell Address," noted that citizens must be adamantly against "the first dawning of every attempt to alienate any portion of our country from the rest." In an 1858 speech prior to the Civil War Abraham Lincoln, borrowing from scripture, recognized "a house divided against itself cannot stand."

John F. Kennedy challenged Americans to accept responsibility for our common plight by asking what we each might do for our country. Similarly, George H. W. Bush celebrated a thousand points of light to acknowledge community good works.

Former Republican senator Jeff Flake understood that pitting Americans against each other isn't wise. He explained why he voted against his party in the 2016 presidential election in *Conscience of a Conservative*: "Anger and resentment and blaming groups of people for our problems might work politically in the short term, but it's a dangerous impulse in a pluralistic society, and we know from history that it's an impulse that, once acted upon, never ends well."

To protect our democracy we, all Americans—Republicans, Democrats, Independents, and everyone else—should be alarmed if a leader seeks to divide us for political gain, especially at the expense of the weakest in society. This would require "stepping off the sidelines."

THE LAND

A democracy is made up of the people, but also the land upon which the people live. This means, in part, homeland security from foreign influence or aggression. In addition, over many decades, we've seen shifts toward a "more perfect Union" through legislation that protects the air we breathe, the water we drink, the health of the land itself, and the myriad other species that inhabit the land.

We should be alarmed if a leader pursued dismantling the Environmental Protection Agency, eroding the role of science in government, reducing the boundaries of national monuments, and compromising protections for endangered species. Further, the American public—of whom the majority believe that the climate crisis is caused by human activity, along with a near-universal consensus among scientists—should be concerned if an administration denied climate science. And we should be further alarmed by expansion of oil and gas production on public lands, while deregulating standards to mitigate use of fossil fuels, and at the same time denigrating efforts toward clean energy sources—all of which exacerbate climate change.

Such practices are counterproductive in a democracy that prizes wise land stewardship and community health, as well as planetary responsibility, so outright hostility toward a wide range of conservation issues should raise a red flag that requires "stepping off the sidelines."

CITIZENSHIP IN A DEMOCRACY

The individual unit of democracy is the citizen, collectively making up the whole of democracy. Citizens have the right to vote in a democracy and further have the opportunity and obligation to participate in civic matters.

I tell my university students that citizenship is a privilege and an obligation. I report that, to my recollection, I've never missed voting in an election and that my hope for them is that, starting now, they can say the same thing when they are my age. Voting is a commitment that we make to ourselves, to each other, and to the common good. Yet knowing how to vote is also critical. I stress the importance of seeking accurate information, studying the candidates and issues, and voting one's conscience. This is especially important in an age when social media can so quickly spread false information.

In 2019, I strived especially so to "step off the sidelines." I don't want to look back with regrets for "saying nothing." I provided comments and signed petitions that pertain to the management of our public lands. I donated money to candidates and causes I believe in that focus on equal rights and thoughtful land stewardship. I wrote letters and made phone calls to my senators and other representatives.

For most of my life I've expressed myself through the press, having written full-length opinion pieces, shorter commentaries, and letters to the editor most recently for the *San Diego Union-Tribune* and the *New York Times*. In 2019, I attended rallies, marches, and town hall meetings.

For better or worse, I tell my students what I do to stay off the sidelines, not so much as a model but as an indication that I'm trying to do my part as a citizen and as a suggestion of a few earnest moves toward civic engagement. I believe that interpreters should feel welcome to do the same, to let audiences know their commitment to this profession and to our democracy.

Although we would not tell audiences how they should vote, we are most certainly obligated to tell them how our interpretive sites relate to our very democracy in terms of the people's history and natural processes we interpret there. And we can tell them how we participate as citizens, such as voting in elections.

INTERPRETERS PROMOTING DEMOCRACY

To promote democracy, in the context of our shared heritage in the places where we work, the interpretive profession advocates for the rights of all citizens and for the health and proper stewardship of the land. Interpreters have the potential for extraordinary influence as collectively we talk to millions of people each day at the various sites where we interpret.

All interpreters can relate their sites to what assists our nation to realize its democratic potential; this is something every interpreter can think about and do. It isn't a matter of "taking sides" but rather advocating for democratic values such as equality, liberty, justice, civility, truth, and patriotism, as well as a healthy land to include air, water, and wildlife, all in the interest of the common good. Who, in a democracy, would want to argue against democracy? And if that were the case, should we not be concerned? Once again, this would mandate "stepping off the sidelines."

Heritage interpreters can inspire audiences toward more active education about our republic and a consequential interest in greater civic engagement. In a very real sense, the interpretation we do of our cultural and natural heritage is essential to our democracy. Through thoughtful interpretation we contribute to keeping the essence of our democracy intact and forming a "more perfect Union."

AFTERWORD

As we consider the legacy of Elijah Cummings—his commitment as a citizen, his passion for our democracy, his ability to make friends on both sides of the aisle, his integrity—may we dwell and act upon this update of his words:

> When we're dancing with the angels, the question will be asked, in 2020 and every year beyond, what did we do to make sure we kept our democracy intact? Did we stand on the sidelines and say nothing?

What happens next is up to me. It's up to you. As citizens in a democracy, it's up to us all.

Interpreting New York City's Missing Towers

May the lives remembered, the deeds recognized, and the spirit reawakened be eternal beacons, which reaffirm respect for life, strengthen our resolve to preserve freedom, and inspire an end to hatred, ignorance, and intolerance.

—From the National September 11 Memorial Mission Statement

Many years ago, I had a late dinner at the famed Windows on the World restaurant at the top of the north tower of the World Trade Center. This was during the winter holidays, and I recall New York City sprawled out below, one of the great cityscape views anywhere, lit up like a million Christmas trees. I also remember the peaceful snow flurries as I looked out the windows, 1,300 feet above the city. However, returning to ground level from so far up, the snow had melted into a light mist of rain—like a veil of tears.

Now the north tower and south tower are gone. This has become the site of the National September 11 Memorial and Museum, listed by Trip Advisor as the number one museum in North America in 2018. The lessons here teach us about courage, resiliency, compassion, inclusivity, healing, hope, unity—a respect for one another, an affirmation of life—lessons especially important right now.

Some thirty years after my dinner at Windows on the World I returned to visit the site, now transformed. I booked tickets for the Early Access Museum Tour, which allows for entry into the museum prior to opening to the public *and* an interpretive tour. This was important to me as it provided a less crowded, quieter, more respectful and intimate experience of the site *and* the expert interpretation of a guide.

THE WORLD TRADE CENTER

The World Trade Center (WTC) would be colossal in scale, including two towers, north and south, each 110 stories, the world record for tallest buildings at the time. The WTC complex (seven buildings in all) was a city within a city, with approximately 12,000,000 square feet of office space. Some 50,000 people worked in the buildings and thousands more visited the complex each day.

The WTC was intended as a tribute to world peace. Minoru Yamasaki, chief architect of the WTC, suggested the site should "become a living representation of man's belief in humanity." In extraordinary ways the WTC was able to do that not just once but twice: in its original form and in the aftermath of its destruction. In both instances was evidence of the human capacity to dream, to aspire, to create, to find unity of purpose.

THE FLIGHTS

The morning dawned crystal blue, cloudless, and radiant with promise. The stunning brightness of Tuesday, September 11, 2001, in New York City conjured fleeting dreams of "man's belief in humanity," a world without grief.

Nineteen men associated with the Islamist extremist group al Qaeda were determined to change that. The morning shattered. Four planes were hijacked and used as weapons intended to destroy American icons of economy and government located in New York City and Washington, DC.

At 8:46, American Airlines Flight 11 crashed into the WTC north tower. Shortly after 9:00, United Airlines Flight 175 crashed into the WTC south tower. In both instances everyone on board and hundreds of people in the buildings were killed instantly, vaporized in a flash. Some who were still alive, sensing no option for escape, jumped from the towers to their death.

At 9:37, American Airlines Flight 77 crashed into the Pentagon. Meanwhile, United Airlines Flight 93 had been made aware of the other events. Passengers and crew courageously fought to overwhelm the terrorists, bringing the plane down into an empty field in Shanksville, Pennsylvania. An operator in contact with a man on the flight remembers his last words to the other passengers: "Are you ready? Okay. Let's roll!" Flight 93 was approximately twenty minutes from reaching Washington, DC, with a likely target of the US Capitol Building. America was under siege.

After the second tower was struck, Beverly Eckert received a phone call from her husband, Sean Paul Rooney, who worked there. He said he was on the 105th floor and was trying to find a way to escape. She asked him if it hurt to breathe all the smoke. He hesitated and she knew he had lied to protect her when he said no. They ceased talking about the futility of escape and started talking about all the happiness they had shared during their lives, all the special times, the fun they had together, the pleasure of each other's company. As the smoke got thicker Sean whispered repeatedly, "I love you." Then Beverly heard the roar of an avalanche. The south tower had collapsed. She called her husband's name over and over into the phone. And then held the phone to her heart.

THE MEMORIAL

Nearly three thousand people died. The magnitude of loss is incomprehensible considering all those killed in the attacks and multiplied by all their loved ones who were affected. Dozens of those killed were planning weddings and dozens of the husbands killed left behind pregnant wives. The actual site of the memorial is the final resting place of victims for more than 40 percent of the families affected; remains were never found of their loved ones.

Of 5,201 entries to the Memorial Competition from around the world, Michael Arad's "Reflecting Absence" was chosen to interpret the loss. He invited Peter Walker, a landscape architect from California, to partner with him. From their memorial design statement, they proposed two large voids that encompass the footprints of the Twin Towers as visible reminders of the absence. Water cascades into the voids—like a veil of tears—and disappears into a secondary void at the center of each pool.

Names are a symbol of our identity, and the names of the victims are considered the heart of the memorial. The major planning challenge was to determine where and how to display the names. Some felt there should be a distinction between the first responders who made the ultimate sacrifice (their valor) and everyone else. In the end the design reflected no hierarchies of loss to respect the value placed on all human life regardless of when or where the deaths occurred. As a measure of full inclusivity all deaths from September 11 are listed, as well as those from the February 26, 1993, bombing that killed six people, as well as deaths associated with Flights 77 and 93. The names are cut through bronze panels that surround the two pools, at about waist height. To read the names, then, you naturally bow your head, an act of reverence. I observed flowers in some names, seemingly random, which I learned are placed within the names on victims' birthdays.

As noted in *A Place of Remembrance*, by Alison Blais and Lynn Rasic (2015), around the north pool are the names of those who were working in or visiting the north tower, those on Flight 11, and the victims of the 1993 bombing. Names listed around the south pool are those working or visiting there, on Flight 175 that crashed into the south tower, casualties from Flight 77 and the Pentagon, those on Flight 93 that crashed into a field, those nearby the WTC who were victims, and first responders who died. In total, 2,983 names. 2,983 lives. 2,983 stories.

In an extraordinarily complex gesture, next of kin of the victims could request that the names of other victims be inscribed next to their loved ones so that coworkers, best friends, siblings, or spouses could be next to each other, on the memorial, in death. A computer program ran an algorithm to accommodate the 1,200-plus "adjacency requests." Names appearing next to each other convey the importance of relationships in our lives. For example, the names of the seventy-three employees of Windows on the World are grouped together.

The surrounding plaza offers greenery, including more than four hundred deciduous oak trees that symbolize the annual cycle of rebirth and that despite tragic events, life forges on. The trees also provide a transition from the bustling and noisy city into the memorial, as does the sound of the waterfalls generating a sense of peace and tranquility in deep contrast to the horror experienced there on 9/11. The sound of the water is soothing in the midst of overwhelming feelings of loss. The memorial opened in 2011.

THE MUSEUM

The museum sits between the two pools and was dedicated in 2014. The exterior is made of glass and metal that reflects and shimmers brightly, intended to inspire hope. Toward the entrance visitors see a photograph of the Twin Towers taken just fifteen minutes before the first plane crashed into the north tower, a reminder of how things were that day, the calm before the storm, and how the world changed in an instant. Throughout the museum one feels the collision of universal human concepts: hate, evil, darkness, death, fear, sorrow, suffering counterbalanced by love, goodness, light, life, courage, hope, healing.

Entering a dark hallway, you experience audiovisual panels showing people who reacted in horror as they watched the planes crash into the buildings. Voice recordings, as here, are used throughout the museum to elicit visceral connections to the terror of that day.

A ramp then descends into the museum as a processional moving into a sacred space. Physical artifacts throughout the museum include a wedding ring, a watch from a passenger on Flight 93, a fire truck on the scene, a stairwell that provided an escape route for some of the survivors, and huge remnants of scorched steel.

An enormous piece of art by Spencer Finch is titled "Trying to Remember the Color of the Sky on That September Morning." The forty-foot-high grid features 2,983 hand-painted square tiles, each a different shade of blue, to honor each of the victims. In the center is a quote by Virgil in which each letter is forged from WTC steel, each weighing approximately one hundred pounds: "No day shall erase you from the memory of time."

One exhibit, "In Memoriam," commemorates the lives of all 2,983 victims. The inner chamber provides interactive tables with audio remembrances of the victims by their loved ones. The surrounding walls show the faces and names of all who were lost. The sheer volume of faces returning one's gaze is devastating, the scale of loss overwhelming.

AFTERWORD

In the immediate aftermath of 9/11, people were nicer to each other. Americans were more united. As we reflect on those times, we are forced to admit that we aren't doing so well right now. How would those who lost their lives want to imagine America now after attacks that brought us so much closer together initially?

What do we owe their memories?

Interpreting Hope

Freeman Tilden suggested, in his Fifth Principle of Interpretation, "Interpretation should aim to present a whole rather than a part." I will embrace this principle as I approach this topic. Blind optimism is not the answer. As the saying goes, if you aren't concerned about the current state of affairs, then you aren't paying attention. We need more people paying attention.

Climate heating events including drought, wildfires, heat waves, severe storms, floods, glacial melt, and rising sea levels are impacting billions of people, along with myriad other life forms on the planet. These events have amplified and accelerated, and unless serious action is taken will continue to get worse and increase in frequency.

The coronavirus pandemic killed millions of people worldwide and counting. The war in Ukraine continues and has threatened to go nuclear. There have been mounting geopolitical imbalances, cyberattacks, violations of human rights, displacements of people around the world, global hunger and suffering, and a decline in biodiversity. Microplastics are everywhere, including our bodies.

The United States currently faces political and social unrest, widening economic inequality, a crisis facing those experiencing homelessness, an increase in hate crimes, widespread poverty, mass shootings, and a decrease in life expectancy.

We have a former president facing criminal charges on a wide range of counts who is fomenting turmoil and a congresswoman from Georgia who has suggested a "national divorce" whereby the "United" States would be split into blue states and red states. Other ideological extremists have called for violence and another civil war.

At the same time, we have some states banning books, infringing on human rights, attacking science, and placing restrictions on education to water down a complete and honest telling of the nation's story. The amount of disinformation swirling around us is unprecedented. Many seem to be lost in a sea of unknowingness and despair.

The stress and uncertainty implode among us and often present as physical pain. Nicholas Kristof, a *New York Times* columnist, in a 2023 piece titled "Why So Many Americans Are Feeling More Pain," noted the physical consequences that correlate with the times we are living in—chronic pain arising from emotional discomfort. Kristof wrote, "Americans die from deaths of despair—drugs, alcohol and suicide—at a rate of more than a quarter-million a year, and the number of walking wounded is far greater." It could get worse.

Historian Adam Tooze at Columbia popularized the term "polycrisis." Various crises that would appear disparate are, according to Tooze, deeply entangled and cause more damage than the sum of the parts. If several major problems reach a critical stage at the same time, then this exacerbates disaster. Confronting many global risks at once limits the ability, resiliency, and adaptability of societies to solve the problems. A polycrisis, then, is a domino effect of cascading crises. By all reckonings our plight appears hopeless and perhaps it is.

"IT'S THE END OF THE WORLD AS WE KNOW IT (AND I FEEL FINE)" —R.E.M.

We are struck by a paradox summed up in the book titles of two of my favorite authors, Barry Lopez (*Embrace Fearlessly the Burning World*) and Terry Tempest Williams (*Finding Beauty in a Broken World*). In other words, we find this conundrum of a world in flames that still holds extraordinary goodness and beauty.

As I ponder the disconnect, I'm heartened by the wisdom found in a conversation between activist Tim DeChristopher and author Wendell Berry, published in *Orion* magazine in 2020. At the end of their conversation Berry is explaining how the Shakers were sure the world could end at any time, but "still saved the seeds and figured out how to make better diets for old people."

Then Berry shares something that Thomas Merton, also interested in the Shakers, told him. Merton said, "If you know the world could end at any minute, you know there's no need to hurry. You take your time and do the best work you possibly can."

Building on this, DeChristopher said, "That's why the despair is not paralyzing. . . . It doesn't mean that we stop. It means that we live in this moment as fully as we can."

INSPIRING HOPE

In *The Gifts of Interpretation* (2011), Ted Cable and I present fifteen guiding principles for interpreting nature and culture, each of which is associated with a gift—such as revelation, provocation, beauty, passion, and joy. With each of the fifteen principles associated with a gift, how many gifts are there?

The answer is sixteen. The last gift is intentional, a bonus. The gift of hope.

Carol Graham is an economist who studies hope. In a recent article published in *The Atlantic* she points out that social scientists make a distinction between optimism, the belief that things will get better, and hope, the belief that an individual can make things better. In other words, hope involves individual agency, voluntary action, a change in personal behavior, a choice to become involved. Graham and her colleagues have found a correlation between hope and personal well-being, while despair tends to have negative spillover effects. The critical point is that hope requires doing something. Further, we recognize a moral obligation to behave according to long-term consequences.

Understanding that this is what "hope" means—a change in personal behavior—leads us to what entails a "hopeful story"—one that includes a course of action. And the reason hope is so important to interpreters, and their audiences, is because we face a monumental task that requires meaningful change.

Interpreters can inspire hope at any site by offering relevant messages that include what can be done to confront and solve our myriad problems. At some national parks the namesake of the park itself is in jeopardy due to climate change such as Glacier, Joshua Tree, and Sequoia. The connection of the problem to advocating solutions is obvious.

Still, I can't think of an interpretive program that is within the broad realm of cultural and/or natural heritage interpretation that doesn't offer something in terms of recommended action that leads to solutions—from bat programs to scavenger hunts to Civil War history.

For example, a bat program could touch on how bats and humans navigate differently and include a segment on actions to mitigate light pollution. A scavenger hunt could include something plastic, which could foster a discussion on plastic pollution and its impact on our oceans, among other concerns, and potential solutions to the problem. A Civil War program could include a discussion on how the United States sought a "new birth of freedom" (according to Lincoln's Gettysburg address) and ways in which that same vision is important today to promote freedoms to all people.

We know we can't ignore the problems, and interpreters of all stripes carry important input concerning these myriad challenges. Furthermore, interpreters can offer possibilities (modes of action) for audience members to consider for a better world.

I wrote with Ted Cable that the interpreter's role in offering the gift of hope increases during troubled times and we seem to confront increasingly difficult issues. But we have the tools for the task. We wrote, "The beauty of human integrity commemorated in events of the past and the beauty of the intricacies of nature give rise to hope, and these are the tools of the interpreter."

So the gift of hope is a "bonus" that interpreters everywhere can bestow upon their audiences. Concluding interpretive presentations on a hopeful note provides audiences with an optimistic outlook and a sense of purpose despite circumstances.

One area of focus should be promoting a society that values acceptance and understanding and respect for all people. We need to be working together for the common good of survival and prosperity. We can't solve our problems if our energy is directed toward fighting each other. Unity is essential. Common ground may be found in the love that people have for our parks, monuments, historic settings, wildlife refuges, and other interpretive sites. Our plight demands that people work together. Some level of consensus is necessary for a civil, productive, sane future.

INTERPRETERS CAN CHANGE THE WORLD

Interpreters can provide a bonus, something extra, something unexpected, an unforeseen nugget of wisdom about the state of the world, something memorable, a course of action, something that one might stake the future on. The gift of hope.

Interpretive professionals, seasonals, docents, and volunteers interpret to millions of visitors every day. If we provide honest interpretation, tell the full story, but end on a hopeful note on how improvement is possible . . . we can change the world.

AFTERWORD

I have a friend, Jeanette, who is a minister. She has overseen "Earth Care" programs at her various churches for more than a decade. Her personal interest is in addressing climate change. Specifically, she focuses on planting trees. Jeanette's work reminds me of the adage (of which there is controversy over attribution), "If I knew the world would end tomorrow, I'd still plant a tree today."

Jeanette, it seems to me, strives to be fully present to the magical wonder of the world around us, while at the same time being mesmerized by the possibility of a more just and generous future ahead. Tree planting is Jeanette's hopeful contribution to a better world.

What is yours?

References and Notes

A BRIEF PERSONAL HISTORY AND AN INTRODUCTION TO THE STORIES

The books and articles referred to are presented in the order found as follows:

Tilden, Freeman. (1977). *Interpreting our heritage*. Third edition. Chapel Hill: The University of North Carolina Press. Earlier editions of this book were published in 1957 and 1967.

Sharpe, Grant. (1976). *Interpreting the environment*. New York: John Wiley & Sons.

Knudson, Doug, Ted Cable, and Larry Beck. (1995; second edition 2003). *Interpretation of cultural and natural resources*. State College, PA: Venture.

Ham, Sam. (1992). *Environmental interpretation: A practical guide*. Golden, CO: North American Press.

Buchholz, Jim, Brenda Lackey, Michael Gross, and Ron Zimmerman. (1992). *The interpreter's guidebook*. Stevens Point, WI: UWSP Foundation Press, Inc. (Note: Other titles in the Interpreter's Handbook Series include *Signs, trails, and wayside exhibits: Connecting people and places* and *Interpretive centers: The history, design, and development of nature and visitor centers*.)

Strauss, Susan. (1996). *The passionate fact*. Golden, CO: North American Press.

Mills, Enos. (1920). *Adventures of a nature guide and essays in interpretation*. Friendship, WI: New Past Press.

Beck, Larry, and Ted Cable. (1998; second edition 2002). *Interpretation for the 21st century: Fifteen guiding principles for interpreting nature and culture*. Urbana, IL: Sagamore.

Beck, Larry, and Ted Cable. (2010). *Interpretive perspectives: A collection of essays on interpreting nature and culture*. Fort Collins, CO: InterpPress.

Brochu, Lisa, and Tim Merriman. (2002). *Personal interpretation*. Fort Collins, CO: InterpPress.

Brochu, Lisa. (2003). *Interpretive planning*. Fort Collins, CO: InterpPress.

Leftridge, Alan. (2006). *Interpretive writing*. Fort Collins, CO: InterpPress.

Beck, Larry, and Ted Cable. (2011). *The gifts of interpretation*. Urbana, IL: Sagamore.

Lewis, William. (1980). *Interpreting for park visitors*. Philadelphia, PA: Eastern Acorn Press.

Ham, Sam. (2013). *Interpretation: Making a difference on purpose*. Golden, CO: Fulcrum.

Beck, Larry, Ted Cable, and Doug Knudson. (2018). *Interpreting cultural and natural heritage: For a better world*. Urbana, IL: Sagamore/Venture.

Beck, Larry. (2024). Uncomfortable interpretation. *Legacy*. January/February.

Caputo, Paul. (2022). Editor's desk: There's no looking back. *Legacy*. November/December.

Bushman, Parker McMullen. (2024). Beyond comfort zones: Navigating uncomfortable interpretation. *Legacy*. January/February.

Moffat, Tom, and Lynn Cartmell. (2021). Do I smell smoke? *Legacy*. September/October.

Moffat, Tom, and Lynn Cartmell. (2021). Burnout: How do we put out the fire? *Legacy*. November/December.

MOVING BEYOND THE TREELINE

Prologue: First Nations

Source material comes from:

The Dene First Nation website for Thaidene Nëné National Park Reserve: https://www.landoftheancestors.ca/.

The Parks Canada website for Thaidene Nëné National Park Reserve: https://parks.canada.ca/.

A "Special Section" of the *New York Times* titled "52 Places for a Changed World" published January 16, 2022.

Chapter One: Voyageurs

Source material, including extensive information about the fur trade, voyageurs, and their lifestyle includes:

Olson, Sigurd. (1961). *The lonely land*. New York: Knopf.

Nute, Grace Lee. (1931). *The voyageur*. St. Paul: Minnesota Historical Society.

Nute, Grace Lee. (1941). *The voyageur's highway*, St. Paul: Minnesota Historical Society.

Podruchny, Carolyn. (2006). *Making the voyageur world: Travelers and traders in the North American fur trade*. Lincoln: University of Nebraska Press.

Ross, Alexander. (1855). *Fur hunters of the far west*. London: Smith, Elder.

Voyageurs National Park website: https://nps.gov/voya/learn/historyculture/index.htm.

Chapter Two: Paddling

Back, George. (1836). *Narrative of the Arctic land expedition to the mouth of the Great Fish River and along the shores of the Arctic Ocean in the years 1833, 1834, and 1835*. London: John Murray.

Seton, Ernest Thompson. (1911). *The arctic prairies*. New York: International University Press.

Service, Robert. (1940). *Collected poems of Robert Service*. New York: Dodd, Mead & Company.

McCullough, David. (2002). "The Power of Place." *National Parks*.

Chapter Three: Olesen's Place

Information in this section is derived from conversations with Dave Olesen, literature from his outfitting business, and two of his books as follows:

Olesen, Dave. (1989). *Cold nights, fast trails.* Minocqua, WI: Northword Press.

Olesen, Dave. (1994). *North of reliance: A personal story of living beyond the wilderness.* Minocqua, WI: Northword Press.

For the interested reader, Dave Olesen posts a missive once a month, since 2012, on his blog about his life in the wilderness: https://bushedpilotblog .ca/2024/03/.

Chapter Six: A Complete Desolation, A Northern Fairyland

Pike, Warburton. (1892). *The barren ground of Northern Canada.* New York: MacMillan and Co.

Chapter Seven: No Rescue Wilderness

Leo McAvoy and Dan Dustin have written extensively about the no rescue concept in resource management literature such as:

McAvoy, Leo, and Daniel Dustin. (1981). The right to risk in wilderness. *Journal of Forestry, 79*(3).

McAvoy, Leo, Daniel Dustin, Janna Rankin, and Arthur Frakt. (1985). Wilderness and legal liability: Guidelines for resource managers and program leaders. *Journal of Park and Recreation Administration, 3*(1).

Author's Note: Dan Dustin approved the statement I composed about what he might want to convey to his sons if the situation were dire.

McPhee, John. (1976). *Coming into the country.* New York: Farrar, Straus & Giroux, Inc.

Dustin, D. (2022). *The wilderness within: Reflections on leisure and life.* Sixth edition. Champaign, IL: Sagamore.

OTHER STORIES

Barry Lopez: Leading by Story

Beck, Larry. (1989). Conversations with Barry Lopez. *Journal of Interpretation, 13*(3): 4-7.

Lopez, Barry. (2016). Introduction to I, snow leopard. *Orion Magazine.* July/ August and September/October.

Lopez, Barry. (1993). *Crow and weasel.* New York: HarperCollins.

Lopez, Barry. (1989). *Crossing open ground.* New York: Charles Scribner's Sons.

Lopez, Barry. (1986). *Arctic dreams: Imagination and desire in a northern landscape.* New York: Charles Scribner's Sons.

Lopez, Barry. (1990). *The rediscovery of North America.* Lexington: The University Press of Kentucky.

Lopez, Barry. (2019). *Embrace fearlessly the burning world*. New York: Random House.

Lopez, Barry. (1998). *About this life*. New York: Knopf.

Lopez, Barry (2013). Sliver of sky. *Harper's Magazine*. January.

Orion Society. (2020). *Earthly love: Stories of intimacy and devotion*. Orion Society.

Running for Our Lives

Doyle, Brian. (2019). *One long river of song*. New York: Little, Brown and Company.

Reality Matters (with Daniel Dustin)

Caputo, Paul. (2020). Editor's desk: Interpretation in a fact-free world. *Legacy*. November/December.

McFarland, Melinda. (2020). Another way to handle visitors with politics on their minds. *Legacy*. January/February.

Orwell, George. (1949). *1984*. New York: Harcourt, Inc.

Grant, Adam. (2021). *Think again*. New York: Viking.

Keeping Our Democracy Intact

Source material for this essay is from:

Stolberg, Sheryl, and David Stout. (2019). Elijah Cummings dies at 68. *New York Times*. October 17.

Herndon, Astead. (2019). The lives they lived—Elijah Cummings. *New York Times Magazine*. December 23.

Hannah-Jones, Nikole. (2019/2021). *The 1619 Project*. New York: One World. (Some of the material in the 2021 book of this title was originally published in the *New York Times Magazine* in August 2019.)

Flake, Jeff. (2017). *Conscience of a conservative*. New York: Random House.

Interpreting New York City's Missing Towers

Source materials include:

Museum exhibits, interpretive tour, and observations at the National September 11 Memorial and Museum.

Official website: https://www.911memorial.org/.

Blais, Allison, and Lynn Rasic. (2015). *A place of remembrance*. Washington, DC: National Geographic. Note that this comprehensive volume is the "Official Book of the National September 11 Memorial" and includes a listing of all those honored on the memorial. The story of Beverly Eckert and Sean Paul Rooney originally came from a StoryCorps interview of Eckert, her recollection included in this source.

Interpreting Hope

Tilden, Freeman. (1977). *Interpreting our heritage*. Chapel Hill: University of North Carolina Press.

Kristof, Nicholas. (2023). Why so many Americans are feeling more pain. *New York Times*. May 7.

DeChristopher, Tim, and Wendell Berry. (2020). To live and love with a dying world. *Orion*. Spring 2020.

Graham, Carol. (2023). The new science of hope. *The Atlantic*. April 25.

Note: The "other stories" have all been reworked, at least slightly, and originally appeared in themed issues of NAI's *Legacy* magazine in the order found in this book, as follows:

Barry Lopez: Leading by Story. (May/June 2021; Interpreting Leadership)
Running for Our Lives. (November/December 2020; Interpreting Medicine)
Reality Matters. (November/December 2021; Interpreting Reality)
Keeping Our Democracy Intact. (March/April 2020; Interpreting Democracy)
Interpreting New York City's Missing Towers. (March/April 2019; Interpreting Urban Landscapes)
Interpreting Hope. (July/August 2023; Interpreting Hope)

About the Author

Larry Beck, PhD, is emeritus professor at San Diego State University where he received the Monty (Distinguished Faculty) Award for his scholarship and teaching, the university's highest honor. He received the National Association for Interpretation's Meritorious Service Award and Fellow Award (NAI's highest honor). Beck has written extensively in the interpretive field as lead author of *The Gifts of Interpretation: Fifteen Guiding Principles for Interpreting Nature and Culture, Interpretive Perspectives*, and *Interpreting Cultural and Natural Heritage: For a Better World*. Prior to becoming a professor at San Diego State University he worked as a field interpreter at several units of the National Park Service including Denali National Park and Preserve, Alaska. Most recently he received NAI's President's Award for his 2018–2024 "Justice for All" series in *Legacy* magazine that focused on justice, equity, diversity, accessibility, and inclusion issues.